WHAT WE THINK ABOUT
WHEN WE THINK ABOUT
FOOTBALL

WHAT WE THINK ABOUT
WHEN WE THINK ABOUT
FOOTBALL

Simon Critchley

This paperback edition published in 2018

First published in Great Britain
in 2017 by Profile Books:
3 Holford Yard, Bevin Way
London WC1X 9HD
www.profilebooks.com

1 3 5 7 9 10 8 6 4 2

Typeset in Adobe Garamond Pro 10.5/15
to a design by Henry Iles.

A CIP catalogue record for this book is available
from the British Library.

Printed and bound in Great Britain by CPI
Group (UK) Ltd, Croydon CR0 4YY

ISBN 978 1 78125 922 1
eISBN 978 1 78283 389 5

CONTENTS

'I am sorry for the boy or girl, or man or woman, who has not been touched by the spell of this mysterious sensorial life, with its irrationality, if you like to call it, but its vigilance and its supreme felicity. The holidays of life are its vitally significant portions, because they are, or at least should be, covered with just this kind of magically irresponsible spell.'

William James, 'On a Certain Blindness in Human Beings'.

Socialism

WHAT DO WE THINK about when we think about football? Football is about so many things, so many complex, contradictory and conflicting things: memory, history, place, social class, gender in all its troubled variations (especially masculinity, but increasingly femininity too), family identity, tribal identity, national identity, the nature of groups, both groups of players and groups of fans, and the often violent but sometimes pacific and quietly admiring relation between our own group and other groups.

Football is a tactical game, obviously. It requires discipline and relentless training to maintain the fitness of the players, but – more importantly – to attain and retain the shape of the team. A team is a grid, a dynamic figuration, a matrix of moving nodes, endlessly shifting, but all the while trying to keep its shape, to retain its form. A team is a mobile shifting form pitted against another form, that of the opposing team. The purpose of the shape of the team – regardless of possession, regardless of whether you play offensively or defensively – is to occupy and control space. The way a football team tries to control space has obvious analogies with the policing of space or the militarization of space, whether in terms of attack or retreat, occupation or siege. A football team should be organized like a small army: a compact, unified, mobile and skilled force, with a clear chain of command. As many have said before, football is the continuation of war by other means, but the means of football are clearly bellicose: it is about victory (and sometimes heroic defeat).[1]

As Bill Shankly – my boyhood hero and legendary Liverpool Football Club manager from 1959 to 1974 – said, football is about basic things: control the ball and pass, control and pass, all the time. When controlling and passing is combined with movement and speed, where, after each pass, there are two or three options open to the player with the ball, then eventually the team with the ball will score. And whoever scores the most goals wins. It's

as simple as that. But as the late, great Johan Cruyff, said, 'Playing football is very simple, but playing simple football is the hardest thing there is.'

Unlike sports like golf and tennis, or even baseball, cricket and basketball, football is not individualistic. Although there is no doubt that it has a celebrity-driven star-system where players demand and exert ever-increasing amounts of financial autonomy, football is not just about the individual players, no matter how gifted they might be. It is about the team. Football is essentially collaborative. It is about the movement between players who play together and play with and for each other and who make up the mobile spatial web of a team. Now, a team can be made up of truly gifted individual players, like Barcelona, or of less gifted individuals who function together as a fused group, an effective unit of self-organization where each player knows exactly the role they play in the overall formation of the team. I think of teams like Leicester City in the English Premier League in the 2015–16 season (who really gave football back to the fans), or a team like Costa Rica in the 2014 World Cup or Iceland in the 2016 European Championship. With teams like this, the whole is clearly greater than the sum of the parts.

It is no accident that when Jean-Paul Sartre was trying to think about the nature of organization, he turned to football.[2] The free action or activity – what Sartre call 'praxis' – of the individual player is subordinated to the team, both integrated into it and transcending it, where the collective action of the group permits the refinement of individual action through immersion into the organizational structure of the team. What is taking place in an organized team is a never ceasing dialectic between the associative, collective activity of the group and the supportive, flourishing individual actions of the players whose being is only given through the team. What continually compels Sartre's attention is how an organization shapes the relation between individual and collective action, in the constantly shifting, dynamic form of a football team. The individual motions of each player are predetermined by their function – being a good goalkeeper, being a decent central defender, holding midfielder or whatever – but these individual functions find elevation and transcendence in the collaborative, creative practice of a team that plays well together. When a team does not play well together, then collective action collapses into its atomized, individual parts and the whole thing falls apart, players blame each other and the fans turn on individual players. This is bad form, in all senses.

The essentially collaborative nature of football extends to the patterns of sociability amongst the players, and the contrast between the team that plays for each other and the team where each player plays for themselves – the Lionel Messi versus Cristiano Ronaldo dialectic, if you like. To be clear, I am talking about the *formal* sociability of a team as a functioning unit, an effective interactive grid. If a team plays well together on the pitch, then they might get along pretty well together off the pitch. But not necessarily. Some of the players in the World Cup-winning French team of 1998 apparently never talked off the pitch, and the great Eric Cantona was apparently not that sociable when he totally defined the style of Manchester United's Premier League domination of the 1990s. And with the increasing multilingualism and cultural range from which players are drawn (let alone how incredibly young so many of them are), I wonder what they talk about and what they really have in common. But what matters is the formality of the common football language they speak when they play together.

These patterns of sociability find both their echo and their energy in the collective life of the fans (and it is the fans that really interest me. But we'll come back to that). This sociability extends to the very name of the sport that we are talking about: Association Football, which abbreviates into soccer in the United States, although football was very commonly referred to as soccer in the UK until the 1970s before it was later misunderstood as an Americanism. Football is the movement of the *socius*, the free association of human beings, as Marx said in *Capital* (although – sadly – he wasn't talking about football).[3] The reason why football is so important to so many of us is precisely because of the experience of association at its heart and the vivid sense of community that it provides. To push this a little further and admittedly go out on a limb, we might say that the proper political form of football is *socialism*. Freedom is not experienced apart from others, but only in and through association, where collective action both integrates and elevates individual action. To quote Bill Shankly once again – and you can find similar sentiments expressed by the Brazilian legend Socrates, or the Marxist West German 1974 World Cup winner, Paul Breitner,

or the former Argentinian captain Xavier Zanetti – 'The socialism I believe in is not really politics. It is a way of living. It is humanity. I believe the way to live and be truly successful is by collective effort, with everyone working for each other, everyone helping each other, and everyone having a share of the rewards at the end of the day.' Brian Clough, who was a regular on picket lines during the miners' strike in England in the 1980s, said, 'For me, socialism comes from the heart. I don't see why certain sections of the community should have the franchise on champagne and big houses.' As Barney Ronay points out, 'The majority of Premiership clubs have their roots in either a local church or a local pub … A living riposte to the Thatcherite notion that there is no such thing as society'.[4]

Of course, such socialist sentiments seem ridiculous – indeed, positively laughable – especially when we think of the autocracy and sump of corruption that is FIFA, football's governing body based in the bourgeois comfort of Zurich. But such sentimentality also seems risible because of the massive and ever-increasing influence of money in football, where players are encouraged – or, in many cases, compelled – by their greedy agents to act like mercenaries, clubs are the playthings of the super-rich and powerful, and where the devotion of fans is greedily monetized and loyalty is taken for granted at every conceivable moment. And here is perhaps the most basic and profound contradiction of football: its form is association, socialism, the sociability and collective action of players and fans, and yet its material substrate is money: dirty money, often from highly questionable, under-scrutinized sources. Football is completely commodified, saturated in sponsorship and the most vulgar and stupid branding (think of the endless advertisements during Champions League – Heineken in the US, Gazprom in Russia, and so on – and the omnipresence of FIFA World Cup sponsors like McDonalds and Budweiser). It is a monetized and sometimes unbearable spectacle of whatever period of capitalism (late, really late, last minute, or even end-of-days) we are trying to survive through. It can be hideous. And yet I still insist that football is not just that. It is much more. To quote Cruyff again, 'Why couldn't you beat a richer club. I've never seen a bag of money score a goal.' Perhaps what brings us together, as spectators and lovers of the game, is the simultaneous truth and untruth of Cruyff's sentiment.

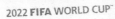

On the one hand, we require a vigorous and rigorous critique of the corrupt transnational corporate structure of football. This could be achieved through a Marxist analysis of the capital flows and inequity in the ownership of the means of football production, or an analysis of power relations in football, in the spirit of someone like Michel Foucault. Such a critique must not shy away from the intrinsic connections between football and violence, football and war, football and colonialism, football and racism, and football and forms of retrograde and atavistic nationalism (as evidenced in the ugly clashes between English and Russian fans in France during the 2016 European Championships, but examples are sadly legion). The need for such a critique is utterly urgent, particularly with the extremely depressing prospect of the next two World Cups being played in Russia and Qatar, in 2018 and 2022, where clearly both decisions were consequences of the systemic corruption of FIFA.

But, on the other hand, football also requires a poetics, more focused on form, that can attempt to evoke its often powerful and deeply moving beauty. As the Argentine coach Marcelo Bielsa (an inspiration to some, like Spurs coach Mauricio Pochettino, and a mad genius to others) says, the essence of football is a gesture at the service of beauty.[5] For there is beauty here: the beauty of the players, the effusive green of the grass intersected with crisp, geometrical white lines; the beauty of the ever-shifting shapes, interconnecting, interlocking movements, dynamic grids and nodal formations on the pitch; and the beauty of the banners and flags waved by the fans and the sound, force and rhythm of their songs. And there is *grace*, an unforced and at times unwilled movement and elegance. I think, obviously, of a player like Zinedine Zidane, especially as he appears in the wonderful 2006 movie by Philippe Parreno and Douglas Gordon, but also of the extraordinary poise and movement of players like Roberto Baggio, Paolo Maldini, Thierry Henry, Andrea Pirlo or Andrés Iniesta. But I also think of the simple grace with which an entire team can move, say, for example, during the first half of Germany's 7-1 *Destruktion* of Brazil in the 2014 World Cup. What was most impressive about the latter was the simplicity of the German play: control and pass, control and pass, move into space, receive the ball, shoot, score.

Association Football is often called the beautiful game without that thought ever going anywhere.

Why is it beautiful and in what does its beauty consist? In this little book, I will use the method of what philosophers call phenomenology to try and give some kind of answer to these questions. Phenomenology is a philosophical tradition that begins in the early twentieth century in the writings of Husserl and finds its decisive existential elaboration in the work of Heidegger, Sartre and Merleau-Ponty. It is very simple: phenomenology is the description of what shows itself to us in our everyday existence. It is the attempt to bring to the level of reflection what we pass over in our largely and happily unreflective lives. It is the attempt to make explicit what is implicit in our experience. This is why Merleau-Ponty describes phenomenology as relearning to see the world. The phenomenological approach will lead us into a poetics of time, space, drama and all the elements of what William James calls 'this mysterious sensorial life' that make up the varieties of football experience. My hope is that this approach will enable the reader to see the beauty of football with slightly different eyes.

How do we negotiate the contradiction between the need for a critique of football and the possibility of its poetics? Can the conflict between the association and socialism of football's form and the rampant capitalism of its matter be resolved? At this point, I could say something cowardly like 'this task is beyond my capabilities in this book'. But that would be too cheap. Rather, I think that the contradiction should just be left open, not so much as a dialectic that defies reconciliation as an open wound that we continue to scratch at the beginning of every match, every tournament, every season. Football is a game that compels and delights us, to the same extent that it exasperates and disgusts us. Delight and disgust are equally justified reactions to the game and they rotate in equal measure in every game we watch. In this book, I want to focus primarily on the delight, on the poetics of football, a phenomenology of the beautiful game.

To be clear, I am not here attempting to write a 'philosophy of football', in the sense of crafting a series of axioms, categories or principles – let alone a system – that one might derive from watching the game.[6] On the contrary, the philosophical tradition to which I feel closest – phenomenology – attempts to do the opposite: to get close, as close as possible, to the grain, texture and existential matrix of experience as it is given, and to allow words to echo that experience in a way that might allow us to see it in a new light, under a changed aspect. It used to be thought that football is hardly a worthy object of philosophical attention, being a popular, low, indeed common and vulgar pursuit (I remember, in 1988, when I was finishing my Ph.D thesis, that I had to be restrained from dedicating it to Liverpool legend, Kenny Dalglish). However, things have changed, and, over the last twenty-five or so years football has established itself as a legitimate subject of serious writing. I am thinking here of the work of Eduardo Galleano, David Goldblatt, Paul Simpson, Uli Hesse, Simon Kuper, Jonathan Wilson, Barney Ronay, Barry Glendinning and very many others, whose writing I have read, respect enormously, and have learnt a great deal from. If I wore a hat, I would doff it in their collective direction.

To my surprise and delight, as I was writing this little book, I discovered that much of what I believe to be true philosophically – about matters as general as space, time, passion, reason, aesthetics, morals and politics – turns out to be most true of

football. Indeed, perhaps these matters are only true of football. Of course, this could either mean that philosophy is reducible to some sort of arguably trivial sport, or that football gives us privileged access to abiding insights into what it means to be a human being in the world. I very much hope that I can persuade the reader that the latter is the case.

Football is a lifelong passion of mine, indeed it is one of the very few things that can be said to bind together that life and link it to the lives of others, some of whom are very close to me, such as my father and son, some of whom are further away (although one of the extraordinary things about football is the way in which it constantly allows you to gain new acquaintances, some of which deepen into abiding football friendships). This book is an attempt to make sense of that passion in the only way I know, through philosophical concepts and texts that seem, at least in my mind's eye, to resonate closely with the experience of football.

I should also confess that this book is not written from a neutral perspective. My only religious commitment is to Liverpool Football Club. All my family came from Liverpool, and although there was an Evertonian wing in my mother's family, LFC always predominated. I was raised with a fanatical devotion to LFC and a belief that my team was not just very good, but that its fans were special and its culture unique. I think it is pointless to conceal my allegiance because such loyalty to team, identity, place and history is a large part of what the experience of football and this book is all about. I am therefore guilty of Anfield exceptionalism. I know how irritating this can be to fans of other teams, because LFC supporters always seem so self-righteous and to think that what happened to them happened first / better / more intensely / more profoundly than elsewhere. This is obviously completely delusional and empirically wrong. When one's devotion to one's team lapses into dogmatism or moves over into verbal and even physical violence, then it is not just that something has gone awry. Rather, the whole point of football has been missed. In my view, as I will try to show, there is an inherent rationality in football that permits both passionately held commitment to one's team at the same time as being able to tolerate, understand and indeed encourage others' deeply felt support of their teams. At which point, when fans of opposing teams meet, an argument begins, often a really interesting argument, back and forth with reasons and evidence on both sides. Football is an argument and the point of this little book is not to settle that argument, but to describe and invite it.

Sensate ecstasy

I WANT TO BEGIN with the idea of a poetics of football. I am borrowing this line of thought from the Belgian writer and artist, Jean-Philippe Toussaint. In 2006, Toussaint published a short, lyrical pamphlet called *Zidane's Melancholy*, and a small compendium of pieces on the World Cup appeared in 2015.[7] His compelling thought is that Zidane's last exit from the stage of football at the World Cup final on 9 July 2006 was marked not so much by the red card of the referee as by the black card of melancholy. However, I find Toussaint's overall approach to football disappointing, short on detail and somewhat passé. The English translation of Toussaint's *Football* was royally skewered by Simon Kuper, who asserts that it is one of the worst books on football ever published, on a par with Ashley Cole's *My Defence*.[8] Given how many awful books have been written about football, particularly ghost-written player autobiographies, this is a considerable achievement. Kuper's point, with which I agree, is that what Toussaint is arguing for – that football should be taken seriously intellectually – is something that has been evidenced in the rise of the increasingly articulate and detailed world of football writing, at least since the time of Nick Hornby's *Fever Pitch* (1992). Toussaint seems utterly ignorant of such developments. I think of publications like *FourFourTwo*, *When Saturday Comes* and, more recently, the truly excellent *The Blizzard*, which are packed with fascinating conceptual and historical meditations on the nature of football, as well as providing a huge archive of deep sociology of the game and its culture.[9] But Toussaint confronts and, I think, to some extent succeeds in articulating a basic problem when it comes to thinking about football: the nature of time. Let me try and explain.

Football opens up a particular dimension in the experience of time. This works best when we're watching live games. When we're watching a game live, we are caught, completely caught, in a suspenseful present. We are suspended in the present of the game, watching the players and the ball move, watching what is happening off the ball, watching the referee, watching

the fans. At each instant of that present, the future is open and uncertain. Anything can happen, even when it sometimes or indeed usually doesn't. We watch and we are drawn into the game, captivated, attentive and, in a word that I will come back to, *pensive*, thoughtfully attentive in a very particular way. We watch in the moment and we await that moment of moments when something extraordinary happens: a sudden burst of acceleration from a throw-in, a fast interchange between players, a defender slips, the attacking player jinks to the right, a space opens, a shot is fired and then there is a goal. A flare detonates somewhere in the stadium. Red smoke scatters over the heads of wildly jubilant fans. People – proper, grown-up, intelligent, thoughtful people, some of them with careers and deep into middle age and even beyond – kiss, high-five and hug each other in delight.

At such moments of moments, we are somehow lifted up, elevated. We try to catch our breath. 'It is happening', we whisper to ourselves. What we have here is what James calls one of the holidays of life, something like an experience of enchantment, where we are lifted out of the everyday into something ecstatic, evanescent and shared, a subtly transfigured sensorium. It is what I call *sensate ecstasy*.

Some people – and many Americans, it must be said – find football boring. This is wrong. And they are boring for believing it. Rather, football is more meditative, more pensive than many other sports. Football is about an experience of submission to the flow of the game. The great Italian *calcio* writer, Gianni Brera, thought that 0-0 was the ideal game, when the opposing teams play a kind of chess, cancelling each other out and achieving a perfect balance and aesthetic harmony. Indeed, particularly given the media obsession with goal-scoring, endlessly replayed in slow motion and from multiple camera angles, the art of defensive football must be defended. Maybe it was because I was a defender myself when I played, but I have always found a strange beauty to watching one team completely nullify another. To call such football 'negative' is to miss out on the dialectical joys of negation and the subtleties of Italian *catenaccio* or door-bolt, where one team completely closes another down. Think about the force and spatial intelligence of Juventus's 'BBC': Barzagli, Bonucci and Chiellini, the ageing backline who combine into the finest defence in contemporary world football. The Italian tradition of defensive football is well known and I think back to players like Baresi and Maldini who both spent their entire careers at Milan, during their football hegemony. Indeed, the beauty of a good team comes from resting its weight on a solid, consistent defence based on a deep understanding between players that can take years to develop fully.

As the troubled and deeply troubling Joseph Bloch, the former goalkeeper and protagonist in Peter Handke's haunting *The Goalie's Anixiety at the Penalty Kick*, says: 'A good game goes very quietly.'[10] The rhythm of football is not the *staccato* of baseball, or indeed skeet shooting, but more of a *legato*, a smooth, emerging and subtle flow of time. Football is also about shifts in the experience of time. These are shifts in the intensities of experience, when time is revealed – when that moment of moments occurs – to be something malleable, plastic and elastic.

This is also true of space. Football is about the interpretation of space. Thomas Mueller, the German attacker and great exponent of the 'False 9', whose primary tactical role is to lurk around the opposition penalty area, is known as *der Raumdeuter*, 'the spatial interpreter' or even 'the space investigator'. In other words, the space of play in football is also a play of space. This is a point that Steven Connor makes in

his excellent book, *A Philosophy of Sport*, whose use of what he calls 'cultural phenomenology' is very close to the spirit of what I am attempting here, except he does it for all sport and not just football.[11] Connor borrows from Merleau-Ponty's remarks in *The Structure of Behaviour* on the markings of the soccer pitch, to show that the field of play is never a mere object. Rather, the space of play permits a play of space that includes, Merleau-Ponty writes, 'the bodily intentions of the players, just as those intentions are pervaded and orientated by the space in which they are to be enacted'.[12] The markings on the soccer pitch call for a certain, determinate mode of action and these 'initiate and guide the action as if the player were unaware of it'. The lines that mark the pitch are effective lines of force that provide a milieu that shapes the action of the players. It is not true to say that the consciousness of players inhabits this milieu, like an ornament on a shelf or a carton of milk in a fridge. Rather, consciousness *is* nothing else but this play, this dialectic between milieu and action. The spatiality of play is, like time, malleable, pliable and ductile.

Football can sometimes be like Beckett's *Waiting for Godot*, where nothing happens twice, in both halves. If I'm watching Liverpool, or, worse, England labouring away in a major tournament, then a game can be a 90-minute anxiety dream, a recurring and seemingly endless nightmare from which we try to awake but can't. It's horrible. But football can also be something else, something like nothing else. Toussaint suggests, with a certain Belgian loucheness, that perhaps the closest analogy to this experience of intensity in football is the sexual act. As philosophers like to say, this is an empirical issue which I will let readers decide for themselves.

So, we are in the moment, watching the game, submitting fully to the present, awaiting the moment of moments, with the future open and uncertain. But at that moment, the past is erased, is continually erasing itself, like a goldfish's memory. The past of a match is quickly forgotten and sometimes hard to remember. This is also why watching recorded games is so different. Sure, watching highlights can be a lot of fun for fans (unless your team was wretched), for coaches (which is important work) and for pundits (which is much less important work). Toussaint's view, which can be rendered in a distinction made by Husserl, the phenomenologist, is that it is in words that we can reactivate the forgettableness of football

and prevent it from simply sinking into a sedimented and speedily forgotten past. Provided that they are close to the matter at hand, the words of poetry or literature can brush up against the experience of football, 'grasp its movement, caress its colours, stroke its charms, flatter its enchantments'. Toussaint calls such a poetics of football 'apotropaic', namely, a kind of magic that can ward off the evils of total oblivion and bad luck.

Perhaps this need for magic also explains why football is such a superstitious sport and players and fans alike are so wedded to so many peculiar idiosyncrasies. In my case, it is the magical belief that if I don't watch Liverpool play, then they will lose. They somehow need me there, watching intently and anxiously in Brooklyn. Portugal's Eusebio used to have a lucky coin in his boot during games. The Swedish player Niels Liedholm at AC Milan used to consult a personal wizard called Mario Maggi. Romanian striker Adrian Mutu used to put basil leaves in his socks. Cristiano Ronaldo places his boots under a bust of his father on matchday. During the 1998 World Cup, the French captain Laurent Blanc used to kiss goalkeeper Fabien Barthez's bald head. Less well known is that the French team used to listen to Gloria Gaynor's "I Will Survive" before every match, which conjures a very strange image of the Gallic dressing room, with towering figures like Lilian Thuram, Marcel Desailly and Zizou himself bursting into song about being afraid, being petrified.[13]

Toussaint's view is that the experience of football can be almost magically evoked through the power of words, into poetic form, which, for him, is closely related to the experience of the seasons, the environment, melancholy, time, and memories of childhood. At its most extreme, Toussaint's thought is that the words that can shape and preserve the moment of the experience of football can save us from death, giving us a sense of continuity with the past and the possibility of a posthumous survival through the words and lives of future fans.

Although it might appear abstract, this line of thought makes sense to many of us at an intensely personal level. In my case, my father was a lifelong Liverpool fan, training at Anfield in the early 1950s before a career-ending ankle injury (which meant that he always wore Chelsea boots for ankle support in later life, although he looked pretty stylish in them). And, to be honest, football was probably the only thing my father and I were able to talk about with any rationality and shared passion. And my primary patriarchal violent act with my son, Edward, was filling his room with Liverpool paraphernalia to ensure that he would support no other team (it worked). Edward reminded me recently that, when he was ten years old, he asked for an Arsenal shirt for Christmas, as they were the best team in England at the time. Apparently, I didn't even reply and bought him another Liverpool shirt instead. And it is a source of almost perverse satisfaction on my part that Edward is a better informed, more loyal, and much more disappointed Liverpool fan than I. Fans from my generation were lucky enough to watch Liverpool in their pomp in the 1970s and '80s, when it would have taken a team from Mars to beat us, as Shankly said. I'd say that about 40 percent of conversations with my son over the years and 80 percent of our texting is about football. I'm not saying that this is right, nor am I particularly proud of the fact, but just explaining what many of us do when it comes to football. And, of course, my unspoken hope is that if my son has children, then they will also be Liverpool fans. So much for dreams of the afterlife.

Well, not quite. Let me confess something I've never mentioned in public. About seven years ago, I went to see the Merseyside derby at Goodison Park between Liverpool and Everton with my nephew, Daniel, and my son. Before the match, I was queuing up to buy food and drink for the boys and a cup of beefy Bovril for myself. About five yards ahead of me, in a parallel queue, I saw what I took to be the ghost of my father. I mean, it was him. I felt sure it was him. I stared for the longest time, but he was facing in the same direction as me and he didn't return my gaze. But the shape of his face, his nose, olive pock-marked skin, his double chin, his hair, his gait. Everything was identical.

I said nothing and gave the boys their stuff and watched the match. We won 2-0 and Steven Gerrard scored. We were happy. In my nephew's car on the road back to Birmingham where he lived, as my son slept in the back seat, I shyly told Daniel my story. He'd known my dad well as a child. He'd seen him too.

De-subjectifying
football

FOOTBALL NEEDS A POETICS to save it and us from oblivion. It requires a phenomenology where, for a few moments, and in those moments of moments, we are free to subsume ourselves in the twisting elaborations of fate – and perhaps the free submission to fate is the only real experience of liberty that is possible for us. So, let me try and make some gestures in the direction of a poetics of football.

I'd like to begin by thinking about the movement of play and the nature of a game. In order to do this, I will lean heavily on Hans-Georg Gadamer's hugely important and influential 1960 work, *Truth and Method*.[14] Gadamer's broader intent in this book is to furnish a way of describing the claims, thoughts and judgements that are made in the arts and humanities in ways that cannot be reduced to or explained away by the methods of the natural sciences. Rather, such claims require a theory of interpretation that will allow, in Gadamer's view, for an entire ontology of the ways in which human beings engage with the world. This is what he calls 'hermeneutics', and the thought that is driving this view is that the kinds of interpretation that we practise in our everyday aesthetic experience reveal the deep and abiding structures of our being in the world.

However, what specifically interests me in *Truth and Method* is the way in which he begins his argument with an account of play. The key and simple point is that it is the game that is played, not the subject who plays the game. Picking up on the remark of Merleau-Ponty mentioned above, play is not a question of individual consciousness inhabiting an objective playing field. In order to understand play, we have to leave behind the language of subjects and objects, consciousness and supposedly lifeless things. The players have to lose themselves in play and not play the game in their heads. The players know that the game is play, and know, moreover, that the game is playful. Yet, the game has to be played with what we might call a playful seriousness. This is what I mean by saying that we need to 'de-subjectify' football. In order to understand what is happening in football, both players and fans need to get out of their heads.

Hence the importance of rules, the seventeen laws that govern the game, from the precise dimensions of the field of play (Law No. 1), to the procedure that must be followed for a corner kick (Law No. 17). The playing field has to be clearly bounded and marked: 18 yards for the penalty area, 12 yards for the penalty spot, the arc of a circle with a radius of 10 yards from the penalty spot drawn outside the penalty area. The laws of the games – even the subtle, hermetic mysteries of the offside rule (Law No. 11) – have to be respected. To be a little Anglo-centric for a moment, this is why we appear to dislike cheating or play-acting or simulating. We seem to hate it when a player falls dramatically to the ground, hands covering his face, after being grazed on the shoulder by a flying elbow (for example the lamentable behaviour of Portugal's Pepe of Real Madrid in the Champions League Final in May 2016, or indeed the spectacular fall to the ground of Brazil's Rivaldo after being tapped with the ball against Turkey in the 2002 World Cup).

That said, cheating is not just wrong, or to be disapproved of, but is an art, an art practised sublimely by the Italian and Uruguayan national teams. I think of the moment when Luis Suarez handled the ball on the line in the 2010 World Cup match against Ghana, getting sent off in the process, but indirectly enabling his team to win in a penalty shoot-out. On 8 March 2017, Suarez also won a decisive penalty by dramatically throwing himself to the ground in the 90th minute of an extraordinary Champions League game when Barcelona beat Paris Saint Germain 6-1 to reverse a 4-0 defeat in the first leg. Or think of the countless moments when a subtly brutal defender like Giorgio Chiellini will foul an opposition attacker by stepping on his foot during a challenge, doing enough to injure the player but going undetected by the referee. Or we could think back to Maradona's 'hand of God' goal against England in the World Cup in 1986, or Thierry Henry's 'hand of frog', his deliberate handball against Ireland in the World Cup qualifier in 2009. The truth is that there is a real pleasure in watching the rules being bent, the laws being pulled to snapping point. Cheating is a subtle, tactical art, that requires both the presence of the law and the act of transgression. Perhaps this is why so many of us like watching fouls again in slow motion. There is beauty in such controlled violence.

Play is play and we know that it is play, but it has to be taken seriously. Even cheating is serious. Gadamer emphasizes what we might call the ease of play, the relaxation of play. In order to play well, the player has to be relaxed, which is the hardest thing, and is what coaches have to instil in their players. It is the truth that lies behind that banal mantra that coaches tell players: just go out and enjoy yourselves. The game of football is best played with a relaxed, serious enjoyment that is not a feeling inside the heads of the players but which is like a sheen or a patina that shines from a team when it plays well.

Play takes primacy over the consciousness of play. Namely, play is not explained through subjective intentions, brain states or biological functions, just as it is not explained away through endless statistics and data. All of these might be necessary causal conditions for play, for the game of football to be possible (being conscious and alert, not being injured, trying to complete as many passes as possible), but they are not sufficient to describe the life of the phenomenon, which is my concern here. No, the purpose of play is play itself. Play is not the expression of some inner, psychological reality. Therefore, as a first step, we need to separate football from our endless fascination with what is going on inside the heads or the bodies of the players, as in the standard, dumb interviewer's question: 'What was going through your mind when you scored that goal?' If the player is playing well, not very much is going on in their 'mind' at all, and this is the entire point: play and not the consciousness of play. If we can begin to distinguish football from our obsession with the brain, consciousness and what is allegedly going on inside our heads, then we can start to appreciate the peculiarity of the phenomenon of football. Whatever 'mind' is in play, it is not in the head, it is out there, alongside the other players and the fans. With them and not apart from them. Perhaps football requires some kind of hive mind, shared mind or extended mind that shines on the surfaces of things, of playthings. This is why we need to de-subjectify football.

What is it like to be a ball?

FOOTBALL IS A GAME of movement, shape and form which is neither objective in any naturalistic sense that could be explained away through the procedures of empirical science, nor it is merely subjective. So, if we need to de-subjectify football, then, in equal measure, we also need to de-objectify it too. What I mean by this slightly ugly wording is that football takes place in the 'in-between'. Football is played in between the realms of subjectivity and objectivity that modernity has spent so much time seeking to rigidify, notably in Kant's laborious, admirable, but ultimately questionable critical project. To borrow the jargon of the influential French philosopher and former naval officer Michel Serres, football takes place and is played in the

Middle Kingdom by 'quasi-objects' and 'quasi-subjects', namely by players who are not defined by their subjective intentions and in a game that is not explained by objective causal powers.[15] In order to understand the phenomenon of play, we do not just need to get out of our heads and our obsession with psychology, consciousness and inner states, we also need to grant a certain life to the things that fill the field of play. For they are far from being mere lifeless, inanimate objects.

If we locate football in the Middle Kingdom, in the in-between of quasi-objects and quasi-subjects, then this gives us a way of approaching the peculiar mixture of reality and unreality that defines the experience of a football match and with which we are utterly familiar, even if that familiarity is rarely made explicit. In other words, football takes place in the realm of phantasy in the strong, psychoanalytic sense. Phantasy is neither make-believe, it is not subjective delusion, nor is it objectively real. It is that which structures and saturates what we think of as everyday life, a life which finds a peculiarly intense articulation in the phenomenon of football. For example, think about the moment when you enter a major football stadium, like Arsenal's Emirates

Stadium in north London or the Stade de France in Saint-Denis, just outside Paris. You enter the ground, try to orientate yourself, walk through wide, windowless, concrete halls lined with over-priced concession stands, and then you walk up to the steps towards the daylight or (even better) floodlights to find your seat. Then you see the pitch and entire stadium: shining, gleaming. It is real, but too real, hyper-real, almost too much. It is like watching a movie in an entirely immersive 360-degree sensorium. It is real and unreal at once. We do not feel inside our heads, but out there in the Middle Kingdom. It is the empire of the senses, the realm of the in-between, sensate ecstasy. We are under the spell of James's 'mysterious sensorial life'.

Which is to say that there is no immediacy to football, no direct access to a realm of pure subjectivity or objectivity. Every aspect of football is mediated and mediation is not some falling away from a purported immediacy, but the very way in which the phenomenon is presented. In other words, football is mediation all the way down. Perhaps football shares these features with cinema, which is at once completely real and completely invented. Both real and unreal. Two in one.

In this connection, we could think about the growing influence of football video games, both in the traditional football homelands, but also in the massive spread of the popularity of the game in territories like North America and Asia. Maybe football looks more and more like a video game as video games look more and more like football. At which point, the line between reality and simulation gets harder and harder to draw. For many spectators and fans, the experience of football is entirely mediated through video games like FIFA, Pro Evolution Soccer and Football Manager. Not just that, these video games are obviously also watched by players: both by kids who use them in order to learn or hone skills they can put into effect in matches, and by established players, like Messi, Pirlo and Zlatan Ibrahimovic, who confess to spending many hours watching simulations of others and themselves. During the 2014 World Cup, Paul Pogba was seen playing Football Manager and coaching Chelsea. He signed himself to his own team.[16]

To watch a football game is like entering an animistic universe where everything is alive, everything is endowed with some kind of soul: the players, their jerseys, the pitch, the scarves, flags

and banners waving, the huge television screens at the grounds where you can watch the replays. And again, this soul is not some entity inside the head or beneath the heart. It is *ensouled* on the surfaces that we watch. Everything seems alive. Even the ball seems alive. The ball seems to animate itself and to possess an intelligence and awareness. It is a quasi-object, full of subjective investment, hovering between the animate and the inanimate.

Let me pause here and say something a little weird, borrowing from a text written by D. Graham Burnett.[17] Burnett quotes Don DeLlilo when he writes (admittedly, he is thinking about American Football), 'The football knew that this is a football game. It knew that it was the centre of the game. It was aware of its own footballness.' Now, obviously, objectively this is false. The ball is just a sphere of synthetic plastic patches full of air, of a circumference between 68 and 70 centimetres, weighing between 410 and 450 grams (this is Law No. 2). Yet, the ball feels alive when we are playing or watching. Indeed, it feels like it has a life of its own with which the great player has to commune in play. There is an extraordinary moment in the commentary that Zidane gives to Parreno and Gordon's movie, when he says that he remembers one moment when he received the ball and he knew exactly what was going to happen. Zidane knew and the ball knew that he would score before the ball had even touched his foot. Zidane adds that this only happened once, but I doubt it. Ball and player seem to possess a co-intelligence based on their shared life. That said, even great players can be made to look stupid by the ball, as it slips inexplicably from a goalie's hands, slides under the foot that attempts to trap it, or allows itself to be hoisted high over the crossbar instead of buried in the net by a striker six yards from goal. And it is a startling, indeed comical, fact that the precise composition of the ball changes for every World Cup, with Adidas introducing some brilliant new technical innovation for each tournament. Which means that players have difficulty controlling the ball and commentators spend hours discussing it.

In 1974, Thomas Nagel wrote one of the most discussed papers on the problem of consciousness in the last half-century, 'What Is It Like to Be a Bat?'[18] But What Is It Like to Be a Ball? Let me risk a further speculation here. The ball is like a dummy, a ventriloquist's dummy. Now, we know that a dummy is empirically, objectively, just a piece of wood, covered in rags, with someone's hand up its ass. It is not alive. And yet the dummy feels alive when it speaks, just as the ball feels alive when we are playing. But the strange thing about the dummy is that even when it is not being animated by the ventriloquist and is just lying unused and ignored in an attic, it still feels like it has a potential for life, a terrifying potential, which is why puppets are such sources of uncanny fear, hovering somewhere between life and death, occupying neither one realm nor the other. We might say something analogous about footballs. Even when they lie un-kicked on the floor and tucked away forgotten in a cupboard, they still have the potential for movement and life and it is hard to resist the call they seem to make: 'Come on, take me out, play with me!' The point here is that we ventriloquize through the football. We animate the ball with our life and in animating the ball we animate ourselves, make ourselves feel alive with a particularly intense sense of aliveness. But that aliveness is also shared by the ball, which is perhaps the quintessential quasi-object.

Repetition without origin

LET'S RETURN TO PLAY and to Gadamer. Play is repeatable and has to be repeatable. Each football game is a repetition of the last game and anticipates the repetition of the next. Football is one long chain of imitative acts or mimetic events, which is what makes the end of the football season so hard to bear. There will be no football for months! (Or at least weeks.) This repetition requires recognition on the part of spectators. We recognize that a game is taking place – we walk past a bar and say 'Oh look, there's a match on' – and the game will follow the path of a repetition, subject to certain rules and procedures, like a ritual. Insofar as the game only exists through repetition, each instance of the game, each match, is as genuine as any original. Indeed, it is more genuine. For it is proof of the continued, repeated life of the game. The game goes on. Play continues. In other words, there is no original football match, no unruly Ur-match played in the wet English grass in the fourteenth century, or by Mesoamericans like the Mayans or indeed by the Chinese at much earlier dates. It is not merely accidental that the origin of football is lost (I am sure that before too long petroglyphs will be found somewhere in a cave in the Pyrenees mountains showing people kicking a Bison skin ball, using the beast's bones as goalposts). This is also why the question of the origins of Association Football in England in the nineteenth century, although sociologically fascinating and important, is irrelevant to football's continued existence. Football is not attached by an umbilical cord to its origin.

To put it more formally, the essence of football consists in repetition, in this game, the previous game and the next game. And none of these games is less original than the last. Each game is the expression of the essence of football which consists entirely in repetition. From these repeated acts that are recognized as such by the spectators, we can construct a series, or a series of series, which might begin to constitute a history, or a series of histories,

say the performance of a team during a tournament or throughout a season, or that might permit the comparison between different seasons. We might privilege a particular series and pick it out for heroic treatment, as when a team like Nottingham Forest were undefeated for 42 matches over two seasons in England during 1977–78, only to be eclipsed by Arsenal, who remained undefeated for an entire season in 2003–4 and were dubbed 'The Invincibles', and continued undefeated for 49 matches. But the same goes for a particularly bad season, a disastrous series, as when Derby County went 32 games without a win in 2007–8. The essence of the series is repetition. Football is a constant act of productive mimesis or imitation that reproduces itself in more games. There will always be next season or the next tournament. There is no original, only the reiterated acts of repetition. Football is not only mediation all the way down, its being consists only in reproduction, in endlessly inventive acts of mimesis.

Theatre of identity and non-identity

FOOTBALL IS DRAMA. People say it all the time. With the important caveat that, in my view, football is a truer drama than theatre. If theatre has been sadly ossifying and slowly dying for the past century, despite the heroic efforts of dramatists like Brecht, Artaud, Grotowski, Peter Brook, Richard Schechner, and others, declining into a kind of consolation for liberal sentimentality, then drama lives in and as football. Vigorous assertions of 'The Living Theatre', as with the eponymous group founded in New York in 1947 and who continue to this day, are paradoxical proof that theatre is dying, fulfilling the same destiny as opera. Football is not just the closest analogy to the experience of ancient theatre in Athens or Epidaurus, where audiences for dramatic festivals were possibly as high as 15,000 or 18,000 spectators, it is characterized by the same basic defining trait: *fate*. It is not that football is the only sport, which is obviously untrue, but rather that it is not really sport at all in the usual sense. As the art critic and Liverpool fan, Hal Foster, once said to me, football is the stage where the sometimes obscure operations of *fate* work themselves out, especially national fate, especially when we watch England slouch their way through another international tournament before committing some act of collective suicide, most recently with the 2-1 humiliation against Iceland in the 2016 European Championship. Football is a theatre of identity – family, tribe, city, nation. But it is the presentation of identity in its ever-twisting, complicated, collapsing and doubled-over forms. Football is the theatre of the differentiation of identity that plays itself out with the players and fans enacting their drama watched over by the forces of fate. It is this fateful drama to which we freely submit in watching a game.

Let me give a couple of examples of the differentiation of identity. Firstly, the peculiar case of Ireland, which I owe to Michael O'Hara and Connell Vaughn.[19] The Irish Football Association was founded in 1880 and represented the whole of Ireland, although most of the original football teams were from the Belfast area. This was obviously during British colonial rule. In 1921, after the partition of Ireland and the establishment of the Irish Free State, The Football Association of Ireland was founded in Dublin. The point is that both the IFA and the FAI have claims over the same territory. Nominally and constitutionally, there is no such state as 'The Republic of Ireland'. There is just the island of Ireland, which is the twenty-six counties of the 'Republic' plus the six counties of the 'North'. To call 'Ireland' 'Eire', in the manner of many right-thinking British leftists, is also missing the mark, and is felt to be demeaning to many Irish people. And Northern Ireland is not a sovereign state, but a constituent unit of the United Kingdom, at least for the time being, Brexit permitting. Let's just say that it's complicated, but the point is that when the 'Republic' plays a football match against 'the North', Ireland is playing itself. This is a wonderful example of the differentiation of identity. It happened for the first time on 20 September 1978 and ended, with no intended dramatic irony, in a goalless draw. Of course, the additional layer of irony is that many of the 'Republic's' players were born in England, especially during big Jack Charlton's time as manager. They were often known as 'England B' or 'the plastic paddies'.

Or take the example of Serbia. I remember visiting Belgrade during the 2006 World Cup. I was scheduled to give a talk in the afternoon of 16 June which coincided with the match between Serbia/Montenegro and Argentina. I politely asked for the talk to be moved to the morning so that I could watch the match with my hosts and anyone else who wanted to come along. This was arranged, the talk was given, and we gathered in a simple outdoor restaurant with a large TV. Now, during the preceding month, on 21 May, a referendum for independence had been held in Montenegro and had passed with the support of 55 percent of the electorate. Montenegrin independence was declared on 3 June. So, by the time of the match, the country that was playing in the World Cup no longer existed. To make things worse, after the teams came out on the pitch, the national anthem of Serbia/Montenegro was 'Hej, Sloveni' or 'Hey, Slavs', the old national anthem of the former Yugoslavia, which had disintegrated in war in 1991. So, a country that would no longer

exist was obliged to sing the national anthem of a former country that no longer existed. The ironies of identity and difference were carefully pointed out to me by my hosts. Argentina went on to crush Serbia/Montenegro 6-0. It was a humiliating defeat. I thought that my hosts would be upset. Not at all. They were absolutely delighted as the disastrous, divided precariousness of their national existence had been played out for all to see: how could the team of a non-existent country be expected to play with any conviction, they insisted.

Music must resound

FOOTBALL IS THE PLACE where the drama of national identity and non-identity plays itself fatefully out against a history of violence and war. Now, the true nature of a piece of drama does not reside in the text or the script or the stage directions, let alone in the subjective intentions of the dramatist (the latter can very often be deceptive or even delusional). No, the truth of drama occurs in and as performance. As Gadamer writes in *Truth and Method*, 'A drama really only exists when it is played, and ultimately music must resound.'[20]

This is also true of football. Complex tactical plans drawn up on iPads, or collated in the constantly consulted large black leather binders favoured by Louis van Gaal, quickly become meaningless when the whistle blows at the beginning of the game. Press conferences and interviews with coaches and players are nicely time-wasting distractions. The essence of football is presented in the match, when the game is being played. And, of course, music must resound. Not through the looping, subtle rhythms of Doric odes sung by the tragic chorus, but through the constant, complex choral accompaniment of the fans' singing, which can exert an almost hypnotic effect, both echo and energy of the action on the pitch. (This resounding music of the fans is totally ruined by the horror of PA stadium music, especially inane songs like Queen's 'We Are the Champions' [Lord help us!]. Call me a Taliban reactionary if you like, but I think stadium music should be banned.)

In his first book, *The Birth of Tragedy* (1872), Friedrich Nietzsche makes a famous distinction between two forces that constitute ancient drama, twin drives that find expression in the form of deities: the Apollinian and the Dionysian. The Apollinian is the art of sculpture, the perfection of individual bodily form, which finds expression in the figure of the tragic hero. The Dionysian is the art of music, which is a communion of orchestrated revelry that produces an intense feeling of intoxication or *Rausch*,

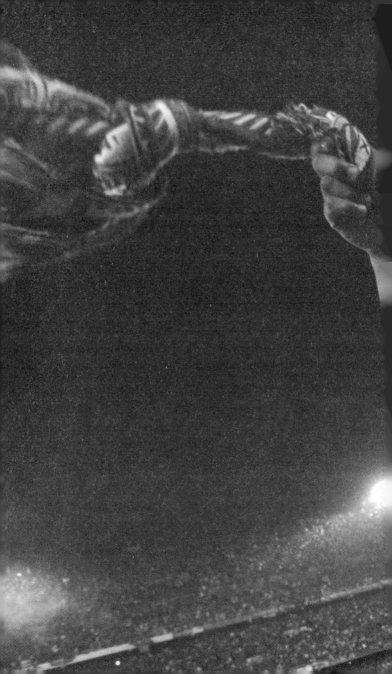

which is nicely rendered in English by the word 'rush'. The emotional effect of music is the rush of togetherness which happens when we are willingly part of a vast crowd, something like a night at the Hacienda in Manchester in the 1980s, or a 1990s Essex rave. Onto this distinction between Apollo and Dionysos, Nietzsche grafts the concepts of beauty and the sublime. The individual, suffering tragic hero gives us the image of beauty, but it is music which is sublime insofar as it cannot be distilled into a visual image, but makes its emotional claim non-imagistically through sound. Although ancient tragedy is the union of these two forces of beauty and sublimity, Nietzsche makes it clear that music is the womb of tragedy, the web out of which it emerges.

This makes perfect sense in relation to football, where the collective song and intoxicating sound of the crowd does not just provide an accompaniment to the beautiful action of the players, but is the sublime matrix out of which play emerges, the force field that energizes the action, taking the form of competitive song and counter-song, strophe and antistrophe. This is why games played in front of empty stadia, say as a punishment for the fans' racist behaviour (which continues to occur with depressing frequency), are such an abomination. A game without fans is a kind of category mistake; a mere training ground exercise devoid of sense. The key to football is the complex, configured interaction between sublime music and the beautiful image, Dionysos and Apollo, the fans and the team. When this works most powerfully, as for example in the extraordinary sound of the Leicester City fans during their home games in the 2015–16 season, generated by voices and simple cardboard clappers slapped in union, or watching the Icelandic fans in the 2016 European Championship with their Viking thunder-clap, the effect can be breathtaking. It can also be funny, as when Manchester United fans adapted the best-known song of a local band, Joy Division, into 'Giggs, Giggs will tear you apart again'.

I attended the Euro 2016 Final in the Stade de France on 10 July 2016 with my son and a couple of his friends. The most memorable feature of a rather dour game was the constant, coordinated and complex singing of the 15,000 Portuguese fans, behind the goal to our left, led by tanned, bare-chested young men beating huge drums. They were a compact, colourful, unified force, starkly different from the rather lame repetitions of *'Allez les Bleus'* from the French fans,

who vastly outnumbered them. Actually, the other powerful memory of that game was an invasion of moths that covered the pitch and terraces before kick-off and swarmed around fans, myself included, as they arrived in their seats. One moth had the audacity to land on Cristiano Ronaldo's face after he went down for the third time with a knee injury. Apparently, the authorities at the Stade de France had decided to leave the floodlights on during the night before the game because of worries about security after the attacks in Paris in November 2015, which began at the Stade de France. It was as if there were some strange, competitive dance between the play of the moths and the footballers, each complimenting the figuration of the other along the frontier of the human and the insect.

Repetition is linked to the phenomenon of the festival, something of which Gadamer was very fond, thinking in particular of the ancient theatrical festival of the City Dionysia, which took place over seven days every March in Athens, where dramas (tragedies, comedies and satyr plays) were performed and music resounded with much pomp. If you had asked an ancient Athenian on their way to the festival what they were doing, they would not have replied, 'I'm going to the theatre', but 'I'm going to *mousike*', which meant words plus music. What is essential for a festival is that it repeats. It marks time. It keeps time. It provides a musical shape to time, defining the rhythm of the year and the movement of the seasons (the City Dionysia in the spring, and the Lenaia in the winter). This is also true of both the annual rhythm of the football season which both punctuates and joins up the weeks, months and seasons of the year, and the quadrennial cycle of European Championships and World Cups (those years without any major championships are, as every football fan knows, wholly depleted in meaning, even if they might prefer – as is the case with me – club over country). It is not the case that there was once an original festival which we simply commemorate, like an anniversary or birthday. Rather, the festival's essence consists in its repeated iteration, in its endless return. The nature of a festival is to be celebrated with regularity, and at a given time. The World Cup must take place in the summer and not in the winter, as with the looming travesty of the 2022 World Cup in Qatar. Personally, I'd like to see Qatar declared a rogue state and the World Cup taken away.

Theory and praxis

LET'S TURN MORE CLOSELY to the spectator. If it is the game that is played and the players have to lose themselves in the play, then the game is played before and for the spectators. So, what of them? For Gadamer, the nature of the spectator is determined by their 'being there present'. Namely, the spectator has to be there present in the theatre, the *theatron*. And this is the meaning that Gadamer gives to the *theoros*, the Greek word for the spectator in the ancient theatre, sitting on wooden benches in a vast auditorium usually shaped from a natural, rocky incline, as in the Theatre of Dionysos in Athens. The *theoros* participates in the drama by being present and giving themselves over to the performance or the game. This participation consists in both attending the play and attending to it, and not being bored or jaded or mystified by the action. It is a participation that requires a kind of self-forgetfulness in what we are watching. We do not watch ourselves, we watch the play and occasionally we become aware of ourselves watching the play.

The spectator sits at what Gadamer calls an 'absolute distance', a distance where they do not take part in the play, or intervene in it by invading the pitch, disrupting or stopping the game, or whatever. Rather, this distance absolves the spectator of direct participation in the play. This is an aesthetic distance or, better, the theoretical distance necessary to see the play and watch the game. So, spectators participate in the play by adopting a theoretical distance from the praxis presented, or the action that is imitated, in Aristotle's formulation: *mimesis praxeos*. They are theorists who participate in the practice of play through sustained acts of attention. This implies that the relation between theory and praxis is enacted in drama and as drama, as the distance between spectator and player, a distance that must never be collapsed into complete proximity or identity. This is another way of thinking about football as a theatre of the differentiation of identity, where the difference here is the distance between theory and praxis. Of course, there is identification of the spectator with the players or with a favourite player, but there has to be distance. The closest that distance comes to collapsing is when a player jumps into the crowd after celebrating a goal and then receives a yellow card. But the game requires aesthetic distance.

We might go further and say that the play exists for the spectator. That is, the game is not for the players, but for us, the fans. Now, for Aristotle, tragedy was a privileged mode of poetics, standing higher than both epic and comedy, and higher indeed than the writing of history. And tragedy existed in order to have an effect on the spectator. Aristotle famously describes this effect in terms of the emotions of fear and pity which are raised or aroused by the drama and achieve catharsis. Gadamer interprets catharsis as purification, which is one of its possible meanings, and this choice of meaning goes together with his preference for seeing ancient drama in terms of a ritual, indeed sacral, communion. The problem with this interpretation is that we have little idea what Aristotle meant by catharsis, and most of the uses of this term elsewhere in his extensive writings refer to organic or biological functions such as menstruation or ejaculation, which might lead to the interpretation of catharsis as a quasi-physical purgation.

This is hardly the occasion to enter into the perennial debate about the meaning of catharsis. Let's just say that it is far from clear that Aristotlelian catharsis can be understood as some idea of ritual purification, let alone sublimation, as psychoanalysts like Lacan prefer, or indeed a kind of moral education, a rather patronizing idea beloved by many philosophers. The idea that catharsis involves some kind of education is understandably attractive as it gives theatre a consoling moral function. Like Guinness, theatre is meant to be good for you. I vigorously disagree with this interpretation and it is profoundly presumptive to imagine that the ancient Greeks required education through theatre. They didn't. Catharsis might have been as simple as the raising and lowering of emotions through dramatic action, after which we feel nothing much in particular, but return to our everyday lives and their many conflicting and banal demands. I think this is closer to the truth, at least with regard to football. We can watch the most exciting, thrilling, pity-and-fear-inducing match, and then – peep, peep – it is full-time and we return to our lives, go back to work, mow the lawn, make a cup of tea and check Facebook. Nothing is fundamentally changed. Life goes on. Who knows, perhaps there will be another match later on? I see no reason to view either drama or football in terms of some idea of moral education. The football fan doesn't need such education because they already know about the game. Sure, they can get to know more, and want to know more, but the overwhelming majority of fans begin from an impressive base of knowledge.

Stupidity

IF THERE IS a sacral dimension to football, then I would rather see it in the very ordinariness of the game and indeed its unquestionable stupidity. Liking football as much as I do – as so many of us do – is really dumb, and part of the enormous appeal of the game is our completely willing submission to something that is pretty stupid. Not to mention taking up a huge amount of time. But I see nothing wrong with being stupid. The sacral quality of football consists in such seemingly silly elements as, say, the colour of football jerseys: the yellow shirts of the Brazilians, the deep, unchanging azure of the Italians, the lily-white of the English, the green of the Irish, the black shorts of the Germans, the heavenly sky blue and black of the Uruguayans, and the Russians who somehow keep changing (during the 2016 European Championships, they were wearing

some kind of maroon as a way of both acknowledging and escaping bold Soviet red, which, of course, looked a lot better). Toussaint speaks beautifully and honestly about these colours, and how they stand out against 'the *absolute* green of the pitch beneath the powerful floodlights of the stadium'.

Philip Schauss nicely teases the stupid out of the world of football by aligning soccer with the figure of Folly in Erasmus's *Praise of Folly*, who just 'blurts out whatever pops into her head'.[21] This is how many fans feel during a game. We will say *anything*. The experience of watching football bestows a strange licence and liberty of speech, a true *parrhesia* or linguistic candour which very frequently veers into the objectionable and completely obscene. The stupidity of football is bottomless, as for example in the obsession with statistics, like the numbers of fouls committed, corners taken, shots on goal, etc., etc., etc. The stupidity of those metrics has been replaced, especially in Germany, with the so-called 'packing rate', which attempts to measure the nature and frequency of passes that move the ball past defenders of the opposing team – this is called *Gegner ueberspielen*, outplaying the opponent – allowing for chances on goal. Schauss writes, 'Fanaticism and obsession are common conditions in football. They stand somewhere between madness and stupidity, without necessarily spilling over into either of the two.' The thought here can also be expressed in terms closer to Gadamer: namely, that to inhabit the field of play, the *Spielraum*, is to enter the blissful stupidity of the experience of losing contact with the usual, everyday world, the world of ends, *die Welt der Zwecke*. In watching football, we enter a different world, a wonderfully dumb world.

I think of the stupidity of the great Brian Clough here, who was famously sacked as manager by Leeds United FC – at that point champions of England – after only forty-four days in 1974. He replaced Don Revie, a hugely successful, tough-minded and beloved manager, who left Leeds to coach England. Clough had made numerous public criticisms of Revie's aggressive, physical style of play, calling them 'dirty' and 'cheating'. I think Clough was wrong here. Sure, Leeds were a hard team, but anyone doubting that Leeds could play football beautifully should look at their 7-0 dismantling of Southampton in March 1972, which is like watching Barcelona play in a mud bath.[22] Amazingly, on the night of his sacking, Clough did a long interview on

Yorkshire Television where the other guest was none other than Revie. Let's just say that the atmosphere was tense. But the key point in the debate between Revie and Clough was when the latter said, 'I believe in a different concept of football to Don Revie. That might be aiming for utopia and it might mean being a little bit stupid. That's the way I am. I'm a little bit stupid regarding this type of thing. I'm a little bit of an idealist. I do believe in fairies.' Despite the cynicism, corruption and chronic capitalism of the game, to be a football fan requires a belief in fairies, a stupidity and a certain utopianism. We could link together the folly of Erasmus's *Encomium Moriae* with Thomas More's *Utopia*, where the latter was the dedicatee of the former. There is a link between folly and the belief in utopia. Clough's utopianism turned on his aesthetic opposition to what he saw as the ugliness of Revie's style of play and a belief in 'carpet football', that soccer is a game to be played on the ground: 'If God had wanted us to play football in the sky, he'd have put grass there'. Clough went on from Leeds to manage Nottingham Forest and won the English league in 1977–78 and the European Cup on two successive occasions, in 1979 and 1980. (The only other English team to achieve this feat was

Liverpool in 1977 and 1978. Milan won back-to-back titles in 1989 and 1990 and Real Madrid did the same in 2016 and 2017.)

Of course, when it comes to international tournaments, the stupidity to which the spectator submits is obviously that of nationalism. Toussaint suggests that football allows an ironic nationalism, a chauvinism with a slightly twisted smile: 'long live Belgium!' As my old friend Philippe Van Haute, who is Flemish, once said to me, the only acceptable form of nationalism is Belgian because the country is so completely divided and is constantly at the point of dissolving. The question is: can such a form of ironic nationalism be sustained when it comes to other countries, such as England or Germany, Brazil or Argentina, Ukraine or Russia, North Korea or South Korea? It is much harder to say. The easy way out here would be to dismiss nationalism and embrace some form of football globalism or soccer cosmopolitanism, whether liberal or leftist. But that seems too easy to my mind and it overlooks the way in which – especially now with the rise of the populist right all over Europe – we are interpellated as national subjects.

Nationhood cannot simply be denied or avoided, for that would be to disavow the fact of where we are from and how that shapes who we are and how we think and speak. Although I am opposed to the simple-minded modern identification of nation with state, I do not think that we can simply choose to ignore or play down the nature of nationhood and its vital importance in providing a sense of place, identity and history. We also need to acknowledge the complexity and exoticism of national sentiment, especially when it is felt for another nation than our own. For example – and I am far from alone in this – my first experience of a passionate attraction to another nation was in 1970, watching Brazil in the World Cup (there is a photo of me aged ten holding a football and dressed in the complete Brazil kit). Football allows me to dream of places that I have never visited and probably never will visit: Cameroon, Kazakhstan, Cambodia … Belgium.

Intelligence

THE BEAUTIFUL STUPIDITY of being a football fan is linked to what Gadamer calls the 'tragic pensiveness' that overcomes the spectator at a drama in the ancient theatre. I think something similar happens in football. The spectator has a pensive distance from the game, a theoretical or aesthetic distance which is the spectator's mode of participation. This does not mean that spectators hold themselves aloof from the action, but participate in it by being there present and constantly attentive. This could be pushed a little further: namely, that the spectator is not in the service of the players or secondary to them. On the contrary, I think that the spectator is the superior party to the parity of the players on the pitch. The spectator is an umpire, a word which derives etymologically from *nonper*, a non-peer, one who is not the equal of others. As

Hegel might have said, if he'd had the good fortune to think about football, the being of the players is not being-in-itself, but *being-for-us*, mediated through the spectators and requiring their recognition in order to affirm the players' existence.

With that in mind, we can expand Sartre's thought, as proposed in the first chapter. It is true that the free activity of the individual player is subordinated to the collective action of the team, both integrated into it and transcending it through the organizational structure of the team. But this collective action or praxis is mediated at a further level through the theoretical gaze of the spectator. That is, it is only through the theoretical recognition of the collective praxis of the team by the spectators that the *totality* of the team can be apprehended as such. The totalization of the team, and indeed the opposing team and the match as a whole, is only granted by the spectators. In simpler terms, the players play, but only the fans see the whole picture. (Although I must say that I am always perplexed by the recurrent phenomenon of fans leaving the game early, five or ten minutes before the end, ostensibly to avoid traffic. I mean, if traffic is your major concern, then why bother going to a game at all?)

There is arguably a need for a distinction between different types of spectators. Namely, between the spectator who was a player and the one who was not. Those of us who are former players – no matter how good, indifferent or crap we may have been – feel the movement of play that is spectated physically. We follow each pass on the pitch with an echoed movement or the imagined suggestion of movement in the body. This might just be the slightest shift in the neck muscles when a cross goes in and you anticipate the movement of the player and maybe mutter 'fucking get in there!' under your breath. This also happens when we watch kids playing football in a park, car park or some such. We become intensely engaged in the movement of play and vicariously engage in it. Indeed, it is sometimes impossible to resist joining in and asking for the ball or engaging in a thundering tackle to get it off one of the kids. This isn't nice, I know.

Now – and this is a key point in the argument and an apparent contradiction – although the spectators have chosen to submit to the beautiful stupidity of football, they are possessed of great intelligence. They know how the game goes and they know how it will probably end. The players lose themselves in

play. If they are playing well, they are lost in the throw and the throes of the match. But the spectator is a thing apart, participating at an absolute distance where they absolve themselves from the frenzied activity on the pitch. Sometimes spectators feel happy if their team is winning handsomely, and feel wildly, if briefly, ecstatic when they score a goal. But often we watch with a sense of foreboding. Pensive distance can be an anxious distance. Picking up on a thought by the classicist Mary Lefkowitz, the role of the spectator is analogous to that of gods in ancient tragedy, observing the action, watching it play itself out, with the foreknowledge that what is played out is not sheer contingency or a game of chance, but part of the larger machination of fate.[23] In ancient drama, especially in Euripides, the gods appeared on a theatrical device like a crane above the stage (the *mechane*), like spectators in a cosmic stadium. Often the players appear like the playthings of fate, unable to affect the course of the drama and alter its often tragic end, despite their intense exertions.

For me, this is particularly the case watching England during a major, international tournament: players fruitlessly buzz about, the ball is endlessly played side to side across the pitch or back to the goalkeeper, attackers are either weirdly static or they run into space where the ball will never come, a tangible sense of fear spreads amongst the players and infects the fans with loathing. The greater the physical effort, the more the players seem to be caught in a spider's web of doom. It's like watching Lucky's psychotic dance in Act One of Beckett's *Waiting for Godot*, that Pozzo calls 'the net'. And the fans have the foreknowledge of all that comes to pass, and sink back in their seats, feeling stupefied and let down. In fact, it is even worse than that, because for as long there is still time in a game, a few minutes of injury time left, we can still hope. As I will show in a while, in football it is not just the disappointment that kills you; it's the ever-renewed hope. The worst thing about being a football fan, especially an England fan, is that horrible, poisonous cocktail of foreknowledge and hope.

Bertolt Brecht had an amazing thought in the 1920s when he was trying to work out the idea for what he called 'epic theatre'. For him, the problem of theatre, particularly in the context of late nineteenth-century and early twentieth-century bourgeois theatrical naturalism, is that the spectator falls into a kind of slumber or state of hypnosis when they go to see a play. What Brecht wanted was an audience that would be awake and intelligent. If the standard theatrical audience just sits there, shuts off its critical faculties and expects to be dumbly moved to tears by the individual brilliance of the actors, then what Brecht wanted was an intelligent, knowledgeable, critical audience. An audience relaxed and expert in its knowledge. This is why Brecht said he wanted something much closer to a sports crowd for his new epic theatre: eating snacks, smoking cigars, talking and making noise, singing, cheering and booing. I think Brecht was right and it allows us to appreciate in reverse the intelligence of a football crowd.

I know this is going to sound odd to those who don't follow football but self-evident to those who do, but I want to claim that there is a genuine intelligence at work in being a football fan. Now, I know what you are thinking. I remember standing on the terraces at Stamford Bridge in the early 1980s and barely comprehending the depth of the racism of the Chelsea fans at the time. It was ugly. I know that when Leeds play Arsenal, the latter's fans delight in telling jokes about Peter Sutcliffe, The Yorkshire Ripper. Manchester United fans make jokes about the Hillsborough disaster of 1989 that left ninety-six

Liverpool fans dead, and Liverpool fans still make jokes about the 1958 Munich air disaster that killed twenty-three people, including eight players from the Manchester United team, and that seriously injured their great manager, Matt Busby. And there are many, many other examples of disgusting tastelessness amongst football fans.

But football fans are not a collection of dumb hooligans, simple-minded nationalists or rabid fascists. Not at all. Nor are they quasi-Nietzschean participants in some sacral, ritual communion. They are an intelligent, often hugely well-informed and critical crowd, even if they are often given to extremes of tastelessness and the licentious candour of *parrhesia*. They are often expert in their knowledge, relaxed in their opinions and never afraid to make an umpire's judgement, say if a player is particularly good or lazy or a coach makes a tactical error. They are an audience that is capable of totality – of seeing the whole picture. I am always hugely impressed by the intelligence of football fans, as much as I am depressed by the ignorance of those who fail to appreciate their wisdom and dismiss it as dumbness. In my view, football is a profound example of discursive rationality. Indeed, perhaps football is the only area of human activity where German philosopher and social theorist, Jürgen Habermas, is right in his claim about the consensual nature of communicative action and the force of the better argument. We support our team and have good reasons to do so. But so do fans of other teams.

There are two features to which I'd like to draw attention: firstly, the rationality of the arguments amongst fans of the same team. I have spent hours, days, weeks and years talking with fellow Liverpool fans, and arguing about the form of the team, the transfer policy, the squad selection, the variety of tactical formations, usually linking this to the history of the team, its traditions, its glories and its glorious failures. When we meet a fan of the same team, there is not just some kind of phatic communion where hearer is bound to speaker through all sorts of non-verbal cues like yelps and grunts. No, we talk, we find out how much they know, what sort of fan they are, and – importantly – how seriously to take them. If you meet a serious fan, and this happens a lot, then you listen to arguments with evidence to which counter-arguments and counter-evidence can usually be provided. So it goes, back and forth, often for very long periods, with a seriousness which is playful

(this is a game, after all) but still deadly earnest. Indeed, we can change our minds about some deeply held passionate conviction about our team. I have experienced it a thousand times, with people of every gender, and all ages, including adolescents and kids; in fact, often with kids, who frequently have a deeply honest, intuitive appreciation of the game. You can have a really decent conversation about football with a ten-year-old. Football lays out easy tramlines for talk and can shift – from word to word – between the inane and the intellectual and back again.

The second feature is the experience of talking with supporters of other teams, perhaps teams that we publicly despise because they are the enemy, like Manchester United. Surprising as it may seem to me, even Manchester United fans have their reasons for supporting them. Even they have their preciously held traditions, histories and folklore. After all, the last time Liverpool won the English league was in 1990 and United have won it no less than thirteen times since that date. Lucky for some. The pain that I feel in response to that fact is tempered with respect, and there are good reasons why it happened. It is not chance. The point is that we can listen to the fan of an enemy team, hear their arguments, listen to their reasons and even change our mind. In my humble opinion, football talk can even be a paradigm for moral behaviour and discussion. If only other areas of life were at once so reasonable and yet so subtended by deep, abiding passion and belief.

Of course, we might wonder why this is the case. Why is it that conversations about football should simultaneously possess the usually mutually exclusive properties of rationality and faith? Why is it that, in relation to football, I can exhibit both a powerful, tribal, visceral loyalty to my team at the same time as showing respect for the enemy, and where the force of the better argument can permit both parties to change their minds? Is it the admission of the basic presupposition of playfulness which permits the seriousness of debate? Is it easier for us to discuss seriously when we know that we are *only* talking about a game?

I must admit that I don't know the answers to these questions. But it is striking when discussions about football and maybe about sports in general, are compared to discussions in philosophy and politics. In politics, clinging to our deeply held prejudices in the face of counter-arguments is perhaps not so surprising. But I remember Bernard Williams saying that, during his long and distinguished academic career, he had only witnessed a philosopher changing their mind on one occasion, which was during a British government inquiry into the nature and effects of child abuse, when the appalling evidence of paedophile pornography had led a moral philosopher to revise their opinion about the need for new parliamentary legislation. I have spent my entire academic career listening to people give papers, thousands of them. On no occasion that I can recall did the response to a speaker take the following form: 'Dr Smith, thank you for your completely convincing talk. You were right. I was wrong'. It never happens. Yet, in relation to the unserious stupidity of football, it happens a lot. Peculiar, no?

Zizou

FOOTBALL IS 'WORKING-CLASS BALLET'.
It's an experience of enchantment. For an hour and a
half, a different order of time unfolds and we submit
ourselves to it. A football game is a temporal rupture
with the routine of the everyday: ecstatic, evanescent
and, most importantly, shared. At its best, football
is about shifts in the intensity of experience,
maximizing those intensities.

My aim in this book has been to try and outline
a poetics of football experience. I'd like to extend
this poetics by focusing on an exemplary artwork
already mentioned a couple of times: *Zidane* by
Douglas Gordon and Philippe Parreno (2006). I see
this film as a homage to Hellmuth Costard's amazing
1971 documentary, *Football As Never Before,* whose
subject was the sublime George Best (whom I saw
play when he was past his best and probably worse

for wear at a testimonial game in the mid-1970s at Luton Town. Although Best didn't move that much, he still did some amazing things with the ball). The subtitle of *Zidane* is *A Portrait of the 21st Century* and these words have a wide range of meaning.[24] *Zidane* is a meditation on the nature of the image and the endlessly mediated quality of reality. We begin the movie by watching the usual, flat TV images and commentary of the game before being sucked into something else … but let's leave that 'something else' for a moment.

At the most obvious level, *Zidane* is a portrait of the twenty-first century, where reality has an utterly mediated quality. It is a world of celebrity and commodity, a world of smooth and shiny surfaces, a hallucinatory reality, nothing more. The twenty-first century is a portrait. Everything is a portrait. Zidane or Zizou himself is a portrait, a perfect and magical fetish, a pure commodity that inspires desire, a product with rights owned by Adidas, Siemens or his whole panoply of sponsors. Zizou is a spectacle.

Sure, you might respond. That's right. Point taken. We are all children of the Situationists, we live in a society of the spectacle and the world is nothing more than a world of commodified images.

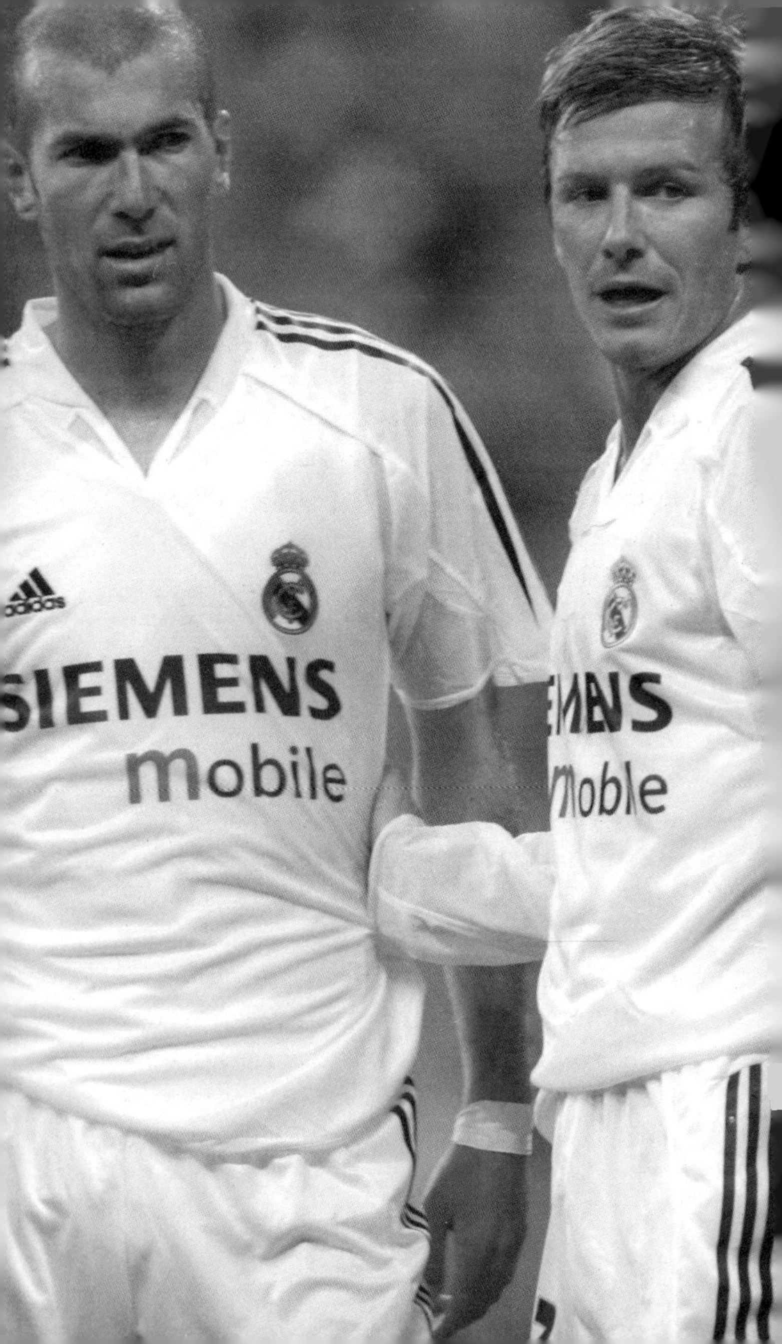
adidas
SIEMENS
mobile

But there is more to the portrait of Zidane than that. Douglas Gordon talks somewhere about the importance of silence and immobility in portraiture. This is crucial, I think. At one level, when we look at a portrait we look for something about ourselves in the image. In an interview he gave to accompany the film, Zidane recognizes this and acknowledges that people watching the film will perhaps be able to feel themselves in his place, *'un petit peu'* ('a little bit'), he adds. Such is the nature of the image at the level of identification. This is fine. But there is more.

It's the *petit peu* that counts. The paradox of *Zidane* as a portrait is that he is constantly in movement and engulfed in the noise of the crowd and the game. And yet, in the firmness, closedness and severity of his face we see through the skin, through the image, to something else, what I want to call some truth, some darker truth, even some reality beyond the image. Somehow, in all the cacophonous noise and ceaseless movement of the film, there is a dark kernel of immobility and silence.

The model for this is the seventeenth-century Spanish painter, Diego Velázquez, and I take it that *Zidane* is a kind of homage to and re-enactment of the famous portrait of Pope Innocent X, that hangs in the Palazzo Doria Pamphilj in Rome, the portrait that obsessed Francis Bacon and inspired his series of studies. (The story goes that when Bacon went to see Velázquez's painting in Rome, he could not bring himself to enter the room, such was the portrait's power over him.) As is well known, when the far from innocent-looking Pope saw Velázquez's portrait, he said *'troppo vero'*, too true, or too much truth. This is echoed in Zidane's remarks on his image in the movie. Firstly, he says that his face looked *'un peu dure, un peu ferme'* ('a little hard, a little closed'), but then he adds, *'c'était moi quoi; voilà, c'était moi'* ('it was me, right; this was me').

Zidane is a portrait in a double sense, then. On the one hand, it gives us a sense of the capture of reality by commodified images in the century into which we have slowly slouched our way. But on the other hand, this portrait is true to Zidane in a way that exceeds the sensible content of the image. There is the suggestion, the adumbration of an inaccessible interiority, a reality that resists commodification, an atmosphere, something like Orpheus looking over his shoulder as Eurydice disappears into Hades.

The film begins with and returns to the phrase 'an extraordinary day'. Of course, Saturday, 23

April 2005, when the film was shot and the match between the mighty Real Madrid and the mightily over-achieving Villarreal (a small city of a little more than 50,000 souls) was played, was a perfectly ordinary day. At half-time we get a flash sequence of random images from the outside world, in a chaotic muddle of the instantly forgotten. All that counts takes place in the stadium, in the face of Zidane. This has something to do with abandoning oneself to chance and the flow of time and the movement of play. As Zidane says, he might have been injured after five minutes or sent off at the beginning rather than the end of the match. The fact is that he wasn't. It is the act of submission to the order of time that is crucial. The 90 minutes of the game provide a frame, an order of counting and accounting within which the extraordinary can happen. Zidane keeps looking up at the clock during the match, checking the time. Such is the time of the line, of the frame, of the game. Vulgar clock-time.

But another temporal order opens up within this submission, a different experience of duration, not the linear flow of 90 minutes, but something else. In abandoning oneself completely to chance, something like necessity begins to appear, even a sense of fate.

This bifurcation in the order of time is also found in what Zidane says about his memory of a match. You don't really remember a game, he says. It's a series of fractured images that announce a different experience of duration: episodic, random, flickering. Memory flares up and catches hold of an image and sucks out its truth. This is time as ecstasy.

In the late 1950s, in the heyday of 3D cinema, there was an experiment in which 'Scratch-n-Sniff' cards were given to moviegoers in order to intensify their experience. At a given prompt, they would scratch away at the card and sniff fresh mown grass, gunpowder, rotting alien flesh or whatever. I can smell this movie, *Zidane*.

There are two things that totally escape you when you watch football on TV: smell and sound. There is something intensely nostalgic – elegiac even – about smell. When I think back to watching games with my dad when I was young or crying in the car home if Liverpool lost (I was a distraught ten-year-old after a humbling 1-0 defeat to second division Watford in the quarter-final of the F.A. Cup in February 1970), then what I remember are smells: the acrid piss stink of the toilets, beefy Bovril, smudges of newsprint on your fingers, cigarette smoke everywhere and the deliciousness of meat pies. Of course, this dates me pretty dramatically and it has all changed. Modern stadiums these days are highly sanitized and more like shopping malls. But there is still the smell of wet earth on the pitch that ascends into the terraces, especially during the winter months. This is the same earth that Zizou treats with such delicacy throughout the match, carefully replacing divots of grass ripped out during play or the persistent light dragging noise of Zidane's foot against the pitch.

Zidane is all about sound. Zidane talks about the experience of sound when he is playing. Of being pulled in and out of the game through noises, of the vast presence of the crowd when you go onto the pitch. He has the most acute sense of hearing during a match. He can hear someone cough or whisper to his neighbour. '*Il y a du son*', 'there is sound', he says, and adds an extraordinary phrase, '*le son du bruit*': the sound of noise. In many ways, this movie is about the *il y a* of sound of noise, the sheer thereness of noise as engulfing. This is what it is to be in a crowd. What I earlier called sensate ecstasy.

We usually know football through commentary, through largely, and hugely, inane commentary. There is no immediacy here. The whole experience is completely mediated and mediatized. Zidane recalls when he was a kid commenting on himself playing as he was playing. According to Laurent Blanc – 'Monsieur Le President' – Pep Guardiola used to do this all the time when they both played for Barcelona in the mid-1990s and he found it intensely irritating. But we all did this when we were kids. We all commented on ourselves kicking a ball endlessly against a wall or whatever: 'The crowd flood onto the pitch unable to contain their joy after Critchley scores the winning goal in the 93rd minute.' It was as if only an act of ventriloquism and self-distancing could grant you access to what was of utmost importance to your being. We can only be ourselves through the voice and persona of another.

The movie *Zidane* gets as close as anything I know to the grain of the game, largely because it is made out of sheer love of football. But we can only get so close. Zidane recalls running and sitting as near to the TV as he could to watch the French TV show, *Téléfoot*, and listening obsessively to the voice of the commentator, Pierre Cangioni. He says – and this is fascinating – that what attracted him was not the content of Cangioni's words, but the tone, the accent, the atmosphere. It is such atmospherics that *Zidane*

tries to evoke, to draw us into, the evocation of space, a heavenly sphere, the time of breath and vapour.

At the end of his peculiar yet utterly powerful short essay, 'On the Puppet Theatre' (1810), Heinrich von Kleist ponders the nature of grace. Given the restless nature of human consciousness, Kleist concludes that grace will only appear in bodily form in a being that 'has either no consciousness at all or an infinite one, which is to say, either in the puppet or a god'. Is Zidane a puppet or a god? I couldn't possibly say. What he has is *grace*. Which means that he could be both. It is the grace of Zidane's movement that is astonishing, even now when he wields his power from the sidelines – usually in a beautifully cut three-quarter length navy blue coat – as coach of Real Madrid.

It is unclear what meaning there is – if any – to heroism in the twenty-first century. The hero is an icon. We know that. But he or she is also something more. The true hero is possessed of fragility and solitude. Most of all, and here is where Zidane comes closest to the figure of the hero, he is wedded to melancholy self-ruination.

Zidane smiles once, maybe twice, in the movie. The second time is towards the end of the match when he exchanges some casual banter with the great Brazilian attacking wing-back with a ferocious shot, Roberto Carlos. Real Madrid are winning after being a goal down to a stupid penalty. Zidane created the first goal *ex nihilo* with an extraordinary show of intelligence, power, speed and skill. He seems happy. But it's a menacing smile. Almost a grimace.

Darkness descends, the eyes darken and he seems engulfed in a claustrophobic intensity of doubt and self-loathing. A teammate is fouled badly, but not appallingly, Zidane runs across the pitch and whacks the guy and looks like he is going to hit him again until David Beckham pulls him off. Then some kind of world of pain breaks over Zidane. He is sent off and submits to the Law, reluctantly, but he submits nonetheless, like at the end of the 2006 World Cup Final between France and Italy (when most of the civilized world was wishing that he had head-butted Marco Materazzi even harder). Heroism always leads to self-destruction and ruination. And it is governed by the black card of melancholy. As Zidane leaves the pitch, he knows that it is finished. He looks helpless. As Kleist says in the final words of his essay on the puppet theatre, 'This is the final chapter in the history of the world.'

Managerial nostalgia

TO TRY AND GIVE a sense of what we think about when we think about football, I have sketched a phenomenology of play, players and spectators. But there is a figure we have left out: the manager or coach. Indeed, Zizou himself has made that difficult transition from player to manager, moving through the ranks from sporting director to B team coach and eventually manager of Real Madrid on 4 January 2016, and winning the Champions League a mere four and a half months later. He won the trophy again with Real in 2017, neatly combining it with winning La Liga for the first time since 2012.

There is a lot of nostalgia surrounding the figure of the manager. This is doubtless one of the reasons why David Peace's books on Brian Clough and

Bill Shankly, *The Damned United* (2006) and *Red or Dead* (2013), have been so successful. Here the manager is presented as a Promethean and brilliant figure, but also wounded, flawed and finally tragic and solitary. I must confess that I find Peace's work hard to engage with, to stay with on the page, although I admire his attempt to give a deeply evocative phenomenology of the manager's stream of consciousness. Part of the appeal of these books to us now, and the lure of the titanic characters they describe, comes from how much the game has changed. Looking back across four decades of neoliberal globalization and rampant capitalism, which has allowed for ever-increasing amounts of money to contaminate football, managers like Clough and Shankly – or indeed the great Sir Bobby Robson, who performed miracles at Ipswich Town and even with England, taking them to the semi-final of the World Cup in 1990 and losing in a penalty shoot against (who else?) Germany – appear as fading memories of a vanished, northern working-class, industrial world; a world caught in grainy black and white images and flickering, jumpy reels of long past games. To this extent, the figure of the manager appears to us now as a kind of traditionalist, defending through his

verbal idiosyncrasies, obsessions and the charismatic power of his personality, the true heritage of the game of Association Football. It is no accident that both Clough and Shankly were self-declared socialists, defending what they saw as the virtue and beauty of the game against both the poisonous influence of money and the cynicism of defensive, route-one football. They both wanted to play the game the right way: on the ground, with attacking speed, movement, skill and total commitment. Our love of figures like Shankly and Clough is a yearning for a purported time before globalization, when the game was simpler and more virtuous. We are in the domain of nostalgia here, but who said nostalgia was a thing of the past? We are also in the domain of myth, but we should never underestimate our need to be seduced by the power of stories about flawed heroes. To this extent, we remain contemporaries of the ancient Greeks.

The manager can appear as a messianic figure, not so much the special one, like Jose Mourinho (who, it must be recalled, got his break with Bobby Robson in Portugal, as his interpreter, and later at Barcelona), as the crucified God, like Clough at Leeds, who was resurrected at Nottingham Forest, only to end his days in disarray. Or as when Shankly mysteriously 'retired' in 1974, left to walk alone and feeling deeply betrayed by his club (Liverpool were clearly to blame for the way he was mistreated). Or the manager can appear as a Lazarus figure, back from the dead. Consider the perplexed and sceptical reaction to Claudio Ranieri's appointment as manager of Leicester City in July 2015, only to win the Premier League by ten points the following May (and then to be sacked – disgracefully – nine months later in February 2017). We could talk about Arrigo Sacchi, the former shoe salesman who transformed the style of European club football when he managed Milan to huge success in the late 1980s. And we cannot omit to mention the great Mario Zagallo, who won the World Cup twice with Brazil in 1958 and 1962, before winning it again as manager of his country in 1970 and as assistant manager in 1994.

There is a kind of puritanism in the figure of the manager, who assumes the role of guardian for austere moral virtues, a person of ethical rigour who gets up early, works consistently and hard, is loyal to his players and devoted to his family, and who also inspires respect, even fear, in his team. Even when the manager enjoys a drink or two, like

Alex Ferguson, or a drink or two too much, like Clough, we like to see the manager as a puritan who is a custodian of the virtue of football, of playing the right way. Beyond any nostalgia, the obsessive commitment to playing the right way and expecting players to fall into line or accept the consequences is something that connects contemporary managers like Mourinho, Arsene Wenger ('the professor') and Pep Guardiola ('the philosopher'). All of them are addicts who clearly find it difficult to sustain an interest in anything outside of football, which is why they are so good at what they do and why we admire them.

For personal reasons that by now will be obvious, the idea of the virtuous and obsessively addicted manager is something that I associate with a lineage of Liverpool managers: Shankly, Joe Fagan, Roy Evans, Kenny Dalglish, Gerard Houllier, Rafa Benitez, but most of all Bob Paisley. Paisley was the most successful Liverpool manager, spending close to fifty years at the club and, during his nine seasons as manager, winning the English League six times, the League Cup three times, the UEFA Cup once and the European Cup no less than three times. After winning Liverpool's first European Cup in Rome against Borussia Moenchengladbach in 1977, he said, 'This is the second time I've beaten the Germans here ... the first time was in 1944. I drove into Rome on a tank when the city was liberated. If anyone had told me I'd be back here to see us win the European Cup thirty-three years later I'd have told them they were mad! But I want to savour every minute of it ... which is why I'm not having a drink tonight. I'm just drinking in the occasion.' Aside from the bellicose, anti-German sentiment, it is the abstemiousness of this response which is so compelling. Paisley didn't want drink to cloud the experience of victory.

Despite the fact that he is German, there is something of this Paisley puritanism in Jürgen Klopp, whom I would now like to talk about in a little detail. I imagine that Klopp is not an unknown figure, and if he is then a simple Google search can yield hours of entertainment. Klopp is a gifted, hard-working, passionate, immensely likeable and tactically astute football coach, who established himself with some success at FSV Mainz 05 in Germany before spending seven seasons at Borussia Dortmund and completely changing their fortunes, winning the Bundesliga twice and getting to the final of the Champions League in 2013. Klopp was appointed manager of Liverpool Football Club on 8 October 2015. My son Edward and I were drinking ale in a pub in London's West End when the news broke. He was completely ecstatic. I was rather pleased myself. Klopp was inheriting a football club in some disarray; one that had lost confidence in the coaching ability of the increasingly delusional and constantly on-message Brendan – 'I once attended a management course and drive a BMW' – Rodgers. The club seemed to have lost direction since the departure of the Promethean Luis Suarez to Barcelona in July 2014 and the failure to win the Premier League in 2013–14, when it was clearly there for the taking. On 27 April 2014, Steven Gerrard slipped on the ball against Chelsea, Demba Ba scored from the error, Liverpool lost 2-0; on 5 May, the next game, with 78 minutes played and 3-0 ahead against Crystal Palace, Liverpool conceded three goals and gifted the Premiership to Manchester City. To put it bluntly, Liverpool choked. The club had also been damaged by a dubious 'moneyball' transfer policy that had led to embarrassments like Mario Ballotelli wearing a Liverpool shirt. We had become a club far too preoccupied with past glories (just to remind you, five Champions Leagues, three

UEFA cups and eighteen English league wins) and arguably mired with a sense of its own victimization. The latter is wonderfully satirized by David Stubbs with the character of the 'Self-Righteous Liverpool Supporter'. I can't resist quoting a few lines,

> There were eleven players on that pitch last night. Pride. Passion. Heart. Commitment. Guts. Honesty. The Shirt. Spittle. The spirit of Stan Boardman. Gerrard. Carragher. All of them, especially the Shirt, were fit to wear the Shirt. They took John Lennon, George Harrison and Brookside from us but they cannot take away our Shirt. What does it represent, the Shirt? To me, to everyone who holds Liverpool Football Club dear, it represents one thing – and that is the Shirt. What Liverpool fan, when they see the Shirt cannot think of the word 'Shirt'? Every letter in that hallowed word counts, every letter, like the Liverpool team, plays its part. Take away the 'r' and what are you left with? 'Shit'. Makes you think, eh? That tells you everything you need to know about the Shirt. Last night, we were Shirt and you know we were.[25]

Perhaps because of their delusional self-righteousness, the patchy form of the Liverpool team in the first games of the 2015-16 season (we were 10th in the league after eight games) had lulled fans into a kind of lacklustre indifference and defeatism. Klopp's arrival changed the mood inside and outside the club very quickly, and although Liverpool's form in the Premier League in the 2015–16 season was marred by inconsistency and defensive weakness, we reached the finals of two competitions, the Carling Cup and the Europa League. Sadly, we lost on both occasions.

I had been invited to speak about football in Basel during the 2016 European Championships, in the first days of July, and immediately accepted. I told the conference organizer, Ridvan Askin, that I would speak about Klopp. I felt at my back the forces of fate like a gathering gale-force wind. Liverpool had embarked on an improbable Europa League run, defeating historic rivals Manchester United, Klopp's former team Borussia Dortmund (we will come back to that game) and Villarreal in the semi-final. The final took place in St Jakob's Stadium in Basel on 18 May and I imagined myself going there and gloating in glory after beating Sevilla. But instead we lost 3-1. Indeed, we were completely outplayed in the second half. I watched the game in a pub in South London this time, also with my son and two of his mates. A goal up at half-time, we looked comfortable. I was wearing my 1976 V-necked, short-sleeved, red Liverpool replica shirt ('the Shirt'), taking a confident piss in the toilet, smiling to myself. I said to the fan standing next to me at the urinal, 'I think we've got the measure of Sevilla and we'll win'. He was more sceptical. He was also right. Seventeen seconds after the start of the second half, following a sadly predictable defensive error by the hapless Alberto Moreno, Sevilla scored and we completely lost our shape and confidence. The midfield seemed to implode, Sevilla's Coke (real name: Jorge Andújar Moreno) scored two more excellent goals and we never recovered or looked like getting back into the game. It was horrible. My son and I could barely speak to each other after the game; we were so disappointed. I flew back to New York the next morning, defeat weighing heavily on me. It still weighs on me ... a bit.

So, Basel was a total failure, a humiliation and capitulation to a better-organized, stronger, more effective and more experienced team. But there is always a lesson in defeat. Football is not just about winning. It is usually about losing. It has to be. But the really strange thing about football is not defeat as such. As I mentioned earlier, it's not defeat that kills you. It's the ever-renewed hope. The hope that every new season offers. The hope that comes in to tickle your feet, and then you realize, as the poet and classicist Anne Carson says, that your soles are on fire.[26] Football can often be an experience of righteous injustice, where defeat is experienced as bad refereeing decisions or a bad pitch or just bad weather. But sometimes your team can simply be outplayed by a superior group of players. That's a different kind of pain, when you realize that your team just isn't good enough. But still ticklish hope flickers and burns.

Klopp-Time

DISCUSSION OF JÜRGEN KLOPP is often defined by banalities: his passion for 'heavy metal football', '*Vollgas-Fussball*' (full-gas football) and '*Gegenpressing*' (counter-pressing), or his being 'the normal one' rather than 'the special one', with his trademark smile. His interviews are always entertaining but not necessarily that revealing. But there is one recurring word in his lexicon that particularly interests me: *the moment*. Football, for him, is about the creation of the moment, what I called earlier the moment of moments. Now, I want to link this to a thought that can be found in Martin Heidegger's most important philosophical work, *Being and Time* (1927), when he talks about the *Augenblick*, the moment of vision or the blink of the eye. I do this not just because Klopp grew up in the small town of Glatten, which is less than a hundred kilometres from Freiburg-im-Breisgau, where Heidegger studied and worked for more or less his entire career; nor because Heidegger was a football fan, with a deep respect for the leadership abilities of 'Kaiser' Franz Beckenbauer, and had a TV hidden in his office so that he could watch games. It is more because I'd like to think about the experience of time in relation to football. As I said earlier, football is about temporal shifts. The shift that particularly interests me begins with clock-time, the vulgar time of everyday life that moves ineluctably from the now of the present and the not-yet-now of the future before slipping into the no-longer-now of the past – tick, tick, tick.

Clock-time finds its confirmation in the linear and chronometric time of the 90 minutes of the match, a time assiduously kept by the referee and his assistants. Contrary to clock-time is what we might call Klopp-time, the ecstatic time of the moment, the blink of the eye, when we are lifted up and out of clock-time into some other experience of temporality. In a crucial moment, quite late in the argument of *Being and Time*, Heidegger brings together a series of concepts that have been developed in the previous chapters of the book.[27] The passage itself is rather complex, so let me summarize. In the moment of

vision, we are carried away in a rapture where we stand outside our immersion in everyday life and truly encounter that everydayness for the first time. In the blink of an eye, we are carried away from clock-time or what Heidegger calls the 'within-time-ness' of the seemingly endless flow of now-points, into an ecstasy where we encounter the world of what Heidegger calls the 'ready-to-hand' and the 'present-at-hand' for the first time. The contrast between the ready-to-hand and the present-at-hand had been developed extensively in the first part of *Being and Time*, and these terms of art describe the two categories under which the world can be apprehended. That is to say, either as the familiar, value-laded, average world of useful things that surround us and with which I have a practical relation, or as a value-neutral world of objects which I inspect theoretically in the manner of a philosopher or scientist.

Heidegger's point is that both these categories of theory and practice become apprehended for the first time as what they are from the standpoint of the *ecstasis* of the moment of vision. To be clear, the ecstasy here is not some sort of Dionysian, drunken intoxication. It is a *resolute* rapture, a sober ecstasy, that sees the indifference of the everyday for what it is and grasps it as a 'Situation', a key concept in *Being and Time*. The Situation is the location where our human 'being there', what Heidegger calls our *Dasein*, is disclosed not as the random happenings of a world seemingly out of our control, but seized hold of as a context for action, rich in possibilities. It is not that we leave the world or ourselves behind, as if Heidegger were simply updating Plato's myth of the cave, but that we see the world and ourselves clearly for what they are and in that moment of vision embrace existence in its manifold potentiality. We are held resolutely in the rapture of the moment. Now, the moment does not last longer than a moment, the blink of an eye. But in that moment, we arrest the flow of clock-time in Klopp-time, and open the potential for another experience of time and thereby create the possibility for history, a history of moments.

Football
historicity

TO BE A FAN is to live for a history of moments, to live with and through a history of moments. To be a fan is to create and possess such a history, or, better, to co-create it and to be able to share and recount it with others and to have the possibility of creating new moments. It is this sharing of moments that allows for the possibility of togetherness amongst fans and binds them into a collective, a community, a deeply felt form of association. In Sartre's terms, mentioned already, this is the passage from the seriality of a line of randomly assorted individuals waiting for a bus or lining up to go to the cinema, to a fused group, a compact and unified force unified by a pledge of loyalty.

Let me fill out this line of thought with the concrete example of a memorable match. In the second leg of Liverpool's Europa League quarter-final game against Borussia Dortmund on 14 April 2016, Liverpool conceded two goals in the first ten minutes and were 3-1 down in the tie overall. Half-time arrived, Klopp disappeared quickly into the dressing room. He seemed very calm, very relaxed, because the performance of the team, in his view, was good and Liverpool indeed created a lot of chances. The key to understanding Klopp's approach to football is not to focus on goals conceded or defeats. Every team will be beaten. What he always focuses on – resolutely, soberly – is the performance, because that is the key to the development of the team. It is the performance that has to be understood and celebrated, not goal-scoring. When Klopp is analysing games with his core coaching staff – 'the brain', assistant coach Zeljko Buvac, and his video-analyst, 'the eyes', Peter Krawietz – he apparently never watches the goals. They are edited out. So, although Liverpool were 3-1 down on aggregate at half-time, Klopp was happy with the performance. He said to the team that they now had the chance to 'create a moment to tell our grandchildren about'; namely, the creation of a history, of what Heidegger would call a heritage whose essence consists in repetition or reproduction, as I tried to show above.

As all football fans know, most games are forgettable and soon forgotten. What we seize hold of, what gives fans their experience of historicity, shared memory and the collectivity of a fused group, consists in a shared series of moments: 1977, 1978, 1981, 1984, 2005, when Liverpool won the European Cup and Champions League. But there are also other moments, like the disgrace of the Heysel Stadium disaster of 1985, which left 39 people dead, nearly all of them fans of the mighty Juventus; or the Hillsborough disaster of 1989, which left 96 Liverpool fans dead at the hands of the South Yorkshire Police. (My cousin David was at the Leppings Lane end of the ground with all the fatalities and – in those distant days before mobile phones – there was no way he could get in touch for more than 24 hours. We genuinely feared for his life.) As every LFC fan knows, the number '96' remains emblazoned on the back collar of the Liverpool shirt between flames of remembrance.

At his first press conference on 9 October 2015, Klopp said with regard to the high expectations that come with managing a big club like Liverpool, 'History is only the base for us … but it's not allowed that you take history in your backpack … This is a great team now. This is the perfect moment to do this.' Klopp knows a good deal about backpacks, as his 1995 sports thesis for his diploma in sports science from the Goethe-Universitaet Frankfurt was called *'Walking – Bestandsaufnahme und Evaluationsstudie einer Sportart fuer alle'* ('Walking – A Taking Stock and Evaluation Study of a Form of Sport for Everyone' – admittedly, not the most thrilling title). There is a strong strand of Heideggerian resoluteness in Klopp as well as an obsessive, even puritanical, work ethic. He continually emphasizes that a team like Liverpool are a great team now, adding the crucial, voluntarist caveat, 'If we want … if we want'. With regard to the pressure of managing a team like Liverpool, he said in an echo of Heidegger on the Situation, 'I feel pressure before each game and between them, of course, but only to develop and improve as quickly as possible. I have to accept the situation.' And again, 'Pressure is there but the art is only to feel the pressure to win games'. What is also central to Klopp and makes his tactical style arguably different from the orchestrated precision of the great Barcelona teams, or the defensive cynicism of certain forms of counter-attacking play, is a particular emphasis on emotion, on feeling, on

passion, on what Heidegger calls *Stimmung* and *Grundstimmung*, attunement and fundamental attunement. For Klopp, although he and his coaching staff obviously use data, football is not just about a biometric or statistical analysis of each facet of the player's game, let alone 'the packing rate'. This would be the error of objectivism in football. But neither is football just about performance, accepting pressure and embracing the situation. Rather, football is about playing with and for emotion, with and for passion, where everything is articulated around the attainment of a fundamental attunement. The task of the coach is to manage this attunement and permit it to flourish in individual and, most importantly, group play; for the collective action of the team to permit the flourishing of individual action and for this to be fed by the energy and music of the fans. Obviously, Klopp is not alone in this emphasis on attunement, whether one thinks of Antonio Conte, Guardiola, Mourinho or Wenger, but the volume is arguably louder and the passion more intense.

Let me risk another analogy with Heidegger, this time with *Angst* or anxiety. Heidegger makes an important distinction between fear, which is always fear about some entity, some fact in the world, and anxiety, which takes nothing in particular as its object. In relation to football, anxiety is not the fear of making a mistake, losing possession, or even losing a game. Anxiety is not jitteriness. No, anxiety is that basic mood or fundamental attunement when our entire being is stretched out into the experience of time, and when we feel ourselves most alive. Anxiety is, importantly, a kind of joy, or what Heidegger calls in his 1929 lecture 'What is Metaphysics?', a calm, a kind of entranced calm. Elsewhere, he also talks about 'the courage of anxiety'. At such courageously, joyfully anxious moments, we are not worried, we are not fearful, we are entirely focused on grasping the situation and on the movement of play. At its best, when one is entirely focused on the game, I think this kind of anxiously entranced calm describes the experience of being a fan. At any second, the moment can come.

Fetching back

THE KEY THING FOR KLOPP is belief. As he says, 'If someone wants to help, you have to change from a doubter to a believer. It's a very important thing.' Of course, going back to the question of managerial puritanism, Jürgen Klopp is a Christian who has not sought to hide his belief in God. When Klopp was asked by my pal Roger Bennett how he deals with the cynicism of the football world with a seemingly fathomless optimism and joy, he replied without hesitation, 'I believe in God and my only job is to do the best in life … My only pressure is to be a good human being.' It is a wonderfully sincere and disarming sentiment, which I have no reason to doubt. The really interesting and perhaps slightly absurd question is the relation between belief in God and belief in a football team. There is no doubt that the concept of the moment that I have tried to describe has a distinct religious cadence. The blink of the eye, the *Augenblick*, is Luther's translation of *kairos* in Saint Paul, the right moment or opportune time when one can make the decision to make the leap of faith in the resurrected Christ. There are arguably many reasons to believe, just as there are many reasons to disbelieve, but the leap of faith is an inherently irrational act, the madness of a decision to see the Situation for what it is, with what I called earlier a sober ecstasy, a resolute rapture. This is what it means to be a fan. As I am not a Christian like Klopp, Liverpool Football Club is the closest I can get to religious experience.

Talking of divine intervention (and, of course, it would be terrific if we could get Jesus Christ on a free transfer from FSV Nazareth 00), let's go back to what happened in the second half against Dortmund on 14 April 2016. It was indeed a moment. After Divock Origi scored for Liverpool to make it 2-1, Marco Reus of Dortmund scored a sublime goal to make it 3-1, creating space on the left side of the pitch before deliciously curling the ball past the keeper with his right foot. I texted 'game over' to my son and slouched back into the couch. But then, nine minutes later, 'the little master', Philippe Coutinho, scored for Liverpool and the mood in the stadium suddenly seemed to change. Everyone could feel it. Forceful belief spread through the fans and the team. The interchange between team and fans grew second by second into a strange, wild but focused intensity. Dortmund could feel it too. Their hitherto dominant midfield began to contract and shrink, their frighteningly fast, counter-attacking movement ceased and Dortmund dropped deeper and deeper into defence. This was possibly going to be one of the great Anfield European nights. Mamadou Sakho scored from a scrappy header on 77 minutes to level the game, but Liverpool still needed an extra goal because of the number of Dortmund's away goals. Then, in the 91st minute, Daniel Sturridge received the ball and moved into space, passed to James Milner, who accelerated towards the goal line, crossed the ball expertly to the back post and Dejan Lovren headed the winner.

Anfield erupted. For a couple of seconds, before he seemed to comprehend what had happened, Klopp was strangely still. It was a moment. He didn't gurn (a gesture which I hate) or do a fist-clenched air punch (an adolescent move which I question, although I do it when watching games alone and it feels so good). The really odd thing is that the winning goal didn't feel surprising. It felt as if it was destined to happen. It felt like fate or the moment of some *deus ex machina*. Thomas Tuchel, Klopp's former assistant and successful successor as manager at Dortmund, described the result as 'illogical'. He was right. Football sometimes defies logic and these are the moments that we live for.[28]

Klopp's post-match press conference was interesting, and it encapsulates much that I have tried to say about the moment, about performance and about emotion, mood and basic attunement. Klopp mentioned that during his half-time talk, he recalled the memory of the moment in 2005 in the Champions League final in Istanbul when Liverpool came from 3-0 behind to beat AC Milan on penalties after extra-time. An obvious reference, perhaps, but effective nonetheless. The point is that the awareness of the history of that moment allows for a repetition or fetching back, what Heidegger would call a *Wiederholung*, in a new historical moment, which itself provides the potential for the creation of future moments, a new heritage. It simply doesn't matter that none of the current Liverpool players were present in 2005, nor that Klopp himself

wasn't there. It is as if the memory of the fans forms a living archive of meaning, a vast historical reservoir that can be drawn from and imbibed. Liverpool's eventual defeat against Sevilla in the Europa League final in Basel is not a refutation of such moments. As I said, there will always be defeats. It is the nature of the game. The question is how a team seizes hold of its history as a way of accepting defeat and trying again, going again, carrying on, together and stronger.

Marcelo Bielsa notes that the function of the coach is to give the team a form and to ensure that a team have style and are responsive to playing in a particular way. The style that Bielsa favours is called 'protagonism', which is the opposite of playing counter-attack, but consists in keeping the ball away from the opponent and decreasing as much as possible their playing time. This is one way to describe the way Klopp got his Liverpool team to play during the early stages of the 2016–17 season. Although the team possessed genuinely talented individual players, what was so exciting was watching the dynamic figurations of groups of players – especially the fluid and beautiful matrix that allowed for fast one- and two-touch interchanges between Roberto

Firmino, Philippe Coutinho, Adam Lallana and Sadio Mane. When Liverpool were playing well then this protagonistic form was clearly visible. When possession was lost, then it was quickly regained, and when a chance was missed, then the team were able immediately to regroup and attack again. Although some of the goals that Liverpool scored were glorious, often the finish or the final tap-in was almost incidental to the formal movement of play, like a full stop that marks the end of one sentence and announces the beginning of another.

So, what went wrong? Liverpool were beset by obvious defensive weaknesses, persistent goalkeeper problems, and an alarming tendency towards periods of sudden collapse, where the team seems to undergo a collective crisis of faith. And maybe this is the fatal flaw with Klopp's approach and its emphasis on passion, which blends all too easily with the way in which raw emotion is privileged in the English game over technique and tactical intelligence. This is not the case in other football cultures – in Italy, for example.

Speaking of Italy, Antonio Conte's Chelsea prevailed easily enough in the English Premier League. They had a tight, reliable defensive structure, fast wing-back play, a better goalkeeper, and the undeniable brilliance of Eden Hazard and Diego Costa. Most of all, what Chelsea exhibited, which is perhaps the most important virtue of a strong team, is consistency and a growing realization amongst the team, the opposition and both sets of fans, that they were not going to lose. And they didn't.

But, there's always next season … right?

Disgust

AS MIGHT HOPEFULLY BE CLEAR by now, I love football. But I very often wonder if I love it too much and this leads me to lose myself and my critical faculties too readily. Perhaps we should be deeply suspicious of football and more critical than celebratory of the role that it plays in our lives. As I said at the beginning of this book, there is a contradiction between the form of football, as association, socialism and collective praxis, and the material content of the game, which is money, in its most excessive and grotesque manifestations. As Bielsa said a few years ago, 'The world of football increasingly resembles the fanatic less and increasingly resembles the entrepreneur more.'[29] I write, admittedly, from the standpoint of the fan, but the success of teams is increasingly judged according to a criterion of corporate productivity: returning

profit on investment to the owners. Now, I don't think this contradiction between the form of football and its matter can be resolved in some way that will enable us to simply feel good about the game. Such was not my intent. Rather, the contradiction is an open, festering wound between form and matter, one that leaves us feeling both delight and disgust at the game, sometimes at the same moment, and especially disgust at ourselves for being so captivated and captured by its spectacle.

Football can be a terrible thing. It is a powerful opiate that sedates the people addicted to it, draining their energies and distracting their attention away from the more important social struggles of their time and place, and incapacitating the potential for political action. Football is without doubt a form of mass psychology that can license the most egregious forms of tribalism at the level of club and the ugliest nationalism at the level of country. Although the empire frequently strikes back in football (as when, say, Algeria defeat France or Ireland beat England), football is a vehicle for the most outmoded colonial assumptions about the relation between the properly patriotic natives and the manifestly inferior and untrustworthy foreigners, between us and them, and we are always better than them. This is something you can find in some football writing, especially when it is wonderfully satirized by someone like David Stubbs in his character of the 'Wing Commander', for whom every international match that England plays is proof of their racial supremacy.[30]

But even when intended as more serious commentary, some football writing suffers from the painful hangover of a whole series of colonial attitudes. A frequently smug and patronizing tone is adopted towards other cultures, whether this is a form of degradation or romantic idealization. And it is important to remember that the romantic idealization of the other, as some kind of noble savage who plays the game in some allegedly more natural and vital way (such attitudes were connected with Brazil in the 1950s and '60s and in more recent decades with African national teams), is itself an expression of their degradation by colonialist discourse. Despite the (hopefully) ineluctable rise in the popularity of women's soccer, particularly in places like the USA, there is no question that football reinforces a whole series of lamentable gender norms and props up a crumbling sense of masculinity, as with the phenomenon of 'laddism' around football in the UK. To oversimplify matters somewhat, one might say that the very structure of the game, with the manager invariably in the role of father surrounded by his loving sons, which is mirrored in the relation between fathers and sons amongst fans, is one of the most powerful testimonies to the endurance of patriarchy. Even when the father/son hierarchy is replaced with metaphors of teacher/pupil or general/soldier, and granting that some football cultures are more democratic – as in the Netherlands where players have long been accustomed to talking back to the boss – football is still deeply marked by paternalism and can tend easily towards authoritarianism.

If football – as Norbert Elias's pioneering and historically detailed work on sports sociology makes clear – offers a micro-sociology of the dynamic figurations of groups that make up wider macro-social formations, then we should not be blind to the iniquitous nature of those formations.[31] On the contrary. We need to be lucidly aware of them. Take the example of violence. Elias tells an engaging, rich and carefully researched story about the role of sport in what he calls 'the civilizing process'. Beginning from the violence of the so-called English Civil War in the seventeenth century, Elias plots a narrative of what he calls 'pacification' where actual physical violence is sublimated into the symbolic contest between opposing parties in the English Parliament in the eighteenth century: Whigs and Tories. For Elias, the process of pacification was intimately bound up with the growing popularity in England of pastimes in the form of sports. Thus, the emergence of sports in England is intrinsically linked to parliamentary government characterized by the peaceful transfer of power from one political party to another. Thus, the codification of sports like football in England in the mid-nineteenth century is an expression of an ever-increasing, ever-widening, process of pacification. Sport is the sublimation of civil war. And football is the peaceful and law-governed continuation of conflicts that found expression in violence in earlier, less civilized, times.

Elias tells a lovely story. A beautiful story. If only it were true. The simplest objection to Elias is that even if he is right about the pacification of violence in England between the seventeenth and nineteenth centuries (and I don't think this is at all self-evident, and there are much more convincing and troubling ways of recounting the history of English class struggle in this period), then political violence is transferred from the homeland to the colonies with an ever-increasing ruthlessness and efficiency. The 'peace' of the homeland is only possible because of the organized political violence of colonization, a process of expropriation which finds its legitimization in the violence of law. Of course, as readers of Walter Benjamin will be aware, this is hardly an original argument. But that doesn't stop it being true. My point is that football is not about the pacification of violence, but is a certain legal organization of violence, a certain colonial codification of forms of social violence that continually threaten to spill over into actual violence, as was evidenced by the rise of hooliganism in England in the 1970s and '80s, a tradition of jingoistic brutality that can be found today in many, many places: Russia, Italy, Ukraine, Egypt, Turkey, the list goes on. From the time of its earliest records in the English medieval period, football was always violent. It remains violent. Football allows us to see the history of violence from which we emerge, but it does not give us anything resembling peace. To paraphrase Raymond Williams, to say peace where there is no peace is to say nothing.[32]

The link between colonialism and the violence of the law can be seen in the very governmental structure which still administers the game of football: The International Football Association Board. Relatively few people seem to know of the existence of this body, founded in 1886, when two representatives from each of the football associations of England, Scotland, Wales and Ireland met in London on 2 June to standardize the laws of Association Football. The Federation Internationale de Football Association (FIFA) was formed in Paris in 1904 and it was finally admitted to IFAB in 1913. Although FIFA is the governing body of football, jurisdictional authority still resides with IFAB. Although IFAB publishes the laws of the game in French, German and Spanish, only the English text of the laws of the game is juridically authoritative. After the partition of Ireland in 1921, as I mentioned earlier, The Football Association of Ireland (FAI) was founded, but it is not represented on IFAB as it is not part of the UK. Interestingly, each of the UK football associations has one vote and FIFA has five votes. Three-quarters of the votes are required for any rule change, which means at least six votes. Thus, interestingly, the support of FIFA is necessary for any rule change, but not sufficient. It still requires support from at least one of the UK associations. An extensive revision of the laws of the game was published on 19 May 2016, which includes a lot of impressive detail, even stipulating the colour of the players' undergarments, which must be the same as their shorts.[33]

Capitalism, commodification, colonialism, nationalism, mass psychology, patriarchy, and the legal codification of violence – this is why I have continually linked delight with disgust in relation to football. To watch and enjoy a game, as innocent as it might seem, is not to be saved from the horrors of the neo-liberal, globalized world, nor is it to be abstracted from them into some higher, sacral realm of ritualized experience. No, it is rather to feel continually compromised by those horrors, those evident wrongs, to be captured within the layers of media and mediation. To watch football is to see our world at its most nauseating and terrifying. Beauty is nothing but the beginning of terror. If football gives us an image of our age, then we see it at its worst, at its most gaudy, in its displays of wealth and financial power. But football doesn't deflect us away from that world. Nor are fans simple-minded dupes of power. They are far from stupid. They know what is happening. They know how the game goes and what it takes, in terms of money, to build and maintain a successful team.

But fans also know that, just for a moment, and in that moment of moments, there can be something more, something that I have tried to describe in this book, which is not about winning but about the attainment of what we might call splendour. At such magically irresponsible moments, there is transport and delight, the form of football gleams above its matter, a dynamic figuration of beauty, the dramatic mobility of play, the movement of free association between players and amongst fans, the spell of sensate ecstasy. At such moments, we hold our breath. Something else, something wonderful, has come to pass. But it passes. We exhale. The horror show goes on.

Endnotes

1 The definitive account of football, politics and war in a global perspective remains Simon Kuper's *Soccer Against the Enemy* (Nation Books, New York, 2006 [1994]). But see also Franklin Foer, *How Soccer Explains the World* (Harper Perennial, New York, 2005).

2 Sartre, 'The Organization', *Critique of Dialectical Reason,* vol. 2 (Verso, London and New York, 1991), pp. 445–504.

3 Marx, *Capital,* vol. 1.

4 Barney Ronay, 'Anyone want to play on the left?', April 25 2007 (*www.theguardian.com*).

5 Professor Juan Pablo Pochettino, 'Marcelo Bielsa hablando de filosofía, estilos de juego y táctica,' 20 January 2010. (*Youtube* video).

6 For a rich, various and interesting collection of essays on this topic, see *Soccer and Philosophy,* ed. Ted Richards (Open Court, Chicago & La Salle, 2010). See especially chapters 30 and 31.

7 Jean-Philippe Toussaint, *Football* (Fitzcarraldo, London, 2016).

8 Simon Kuper, '*Football* promises to be a book no one will like and delivers'. 7 May 2016 (*www. newstatesman.com*); Ashley Cole, *My Defence* (Headline, London, 2006).

9 *The Blizzard* (*www.blizzard.co.uk*).

10 Peter Handke, *The Goalie's Anxiety at the Penalty Kick* (Farrar, Strauss and Giroux, New York, 1972).

11 Steven Connor *A Philosophy of Sport* (Reaktion, London, 2011).

12 Maurice Merleau-Ponty, *The Structure of Behavior* (Duquesne University Press, Pittsburgh, 1965).

13 For more on pre-match rituals and indeed on much else besides, see Paul Simpson and Uli Hesse in their excellent, extremely detailed and very funny book, *Who Invented the Stepover?* (Profile, London, 2013).

14 Hans-Georg Gadamer, *Truth and Method* (Sheed and Ward, London, 1975). See especially, 'Play as a Clue to Ontological Explanation', pp. 106–35.

15 Michel Serres, *The Parasite* (University of Minnesota Press, Minneapolis, 2007). See also Bruno Latour, *We Have Never Been Modern* (Harvard University Press, Cambridge Mass., 1993).

16 Rory Smith 'How Video Games Are Changing the Way Soccer is Played', *New York Times*, 13 Oct 2016. (*www.nytimes.com*).

17 D. Graham Burnett, 'On the Ball', *Cabinet*, Issue 56, pp. 64–72.

18 Thomas Nagel, 'What Is It Like to Be a Bat?' *The Philosophical Review* 83 (4): 435–50.

19 Michael O'Hara and Connell Vaughn gave an excellent presentation called 'Caveman Stuff: Ireland's Soccer Struggle with Identity, Style and Success', at the University of Basel, 1 July 2016.

20 Hans-Georg Gadamer, *Truth and Method*, p. 120.

21 Philip Schauss, 'On Stupidity in Football'; a talk at the University of Basel, 2 July 2016.

22 There are several highlights videos on *YouTube* showing Leeds United's 7–0 defeat of Southampton.

23 Mary Lefkowitz, *Euripides and the Gods* (Oxford University Press, New York and Oxford, 2016).

24 *Zidane, un portrait du 21e siècle*, 2006 (Artificial Eye DVD, 2007).

25 David Stubbs, *Send Them Victorious: England's Path to Glory 2006–10* (Zero Books, Winchester, 2010), p. 139.

26 Anne Carson, *Antigonick* (New Directions, New York, 2012).

27 'In resoluteness, the Present is not only brought back from distraction with the objects of our closest concern, but it gets held in the future and in having been. That *Present* which is held in authentic temporality and which thus is *authentic* itself, we call the "moment of vision". This term must be understood in the active sense as an ecstasis. It means the resolute rapture with which Dasein is carried away to whatever possibilities and circumstances are encountered in the Situation as possible objects of concern, but a rapture which is *held* in resoluteness. The moment of vision is a phenomenon which *in principle* can *not* be clarified in terms of the "*now*". The "now" is a temporal phenomenon which belongs to time as within-time-ness: the "now" 'in which' something arises, passes away, or is present-at-hand. 'In the moment of vision' nothing can occur; but as an authentic Present or waiting-towards, the moment of vision permits us *to encounter for the first time* what can be 'in a time' as ready-to-hand or present-at-hand.'

Martin Heidegger, *Being and Time* (Blackwell, Oxford, 1962), p. 387–88.

28 There are several highlights videos on *YouTube* of Liverpool's comeback against Dortmund.

29 'Marcelo Bielsa – Futbol, capitalismo y valores', 20 October 2013. Posted on *YouTube*.

30 David Stubbs, *Send Them Victorious: England's Path To Glory 2006–2010* (Zero Books, 2010).

31 Norbert Elias, *The Quest for Excitement: Sport and Leisure in the Civilizing Process* (Blackwell, Oxford, 1986).

32 Raymond Williams, *Modern Tragedy* (Stanford University Press, Stanford, 1966), p. 80.

33 See the 200-odd pages of *Laws of the Game,* which make unexpectedly compelling, nerdy reading. (*www.fifa.com*).

Bibliography

Timothy Bewes, '"Form Resists Him": The Event of Zidane's Melancholy', *New Formations,* no. 62 (Autumn 2007), pp.18-21.

D. Graham Burnett, 'On the Ball', *Cabinet,* issue 56.

Anne Carson, *Antigonick* (New Directions, New York, 2012).

Steven Connor, *A Philosophy of Sport* (Reaktion, London, 2011).

Norbert Elias, *The Quest for Excitement. Sport and Leisure in the Civilizing Process* (Blackwell, Oxford, 1986).

Franklin Foer, *How Soccer Explains the World* (Harper Perennial, New York, 2005).

Hans-Georg Gadamer, *Truth and Method* (Sheed and Ward, London, 1975).

Eduardo Galleano, *Soccer in Sun and Shadow* (Verso, London and New York, 2003).

David Goldblatt, *The Ball is Round: A Global History of Football* (Penguin, London, 2007).

David Goldblatt, *The Game of Our Lives: The Meaning and Making of English Football* (Penguin, London, 2015).

Peter Handke, *The Goalie's Anxiety at the Penalty Kick* (Farrar, Strauss and Giroux, New York, 1972).

Martin Heidegger, *Being and Time* (Blackwell, Oxford, 1962).

Martin Heidegger, *Pathmarks* (Cambridge University Press, Cambridge, 1998).

Simon Hughes, *Red Machine: Liverpool FC in the 1980s* (Mainstream, Edinburgh/London, 2013).

Karl Ove Knausgaard and Fredrik Ekelund, *Home and Away: Writing the Beautiful Game* (Harvill Secker, London, 2016).

Simon Kuper, *Football Against the Enemy* (Orion, London, 1994).

Bruno Latour, *We Have Never Been Modern* (Harvard University Press, Cambridge Mass., 1993).

David Macey, 'Un Coup de Boule N'Abolira Jamais...', *New Formations,* no. 62 (Autumn 2007), pp. 15–17.

Tom McCarthy, *Typewriters, Bombs, Jellyfish: Essays* (New York Review of Books, New York, 2017).

Maurice Merleau-Ponty, *The Structure of Behavior* (Duquesne University Press, Pittsburgh, 1965).

Elmar Neveling, *Jürgen Klopp: The Biography* (Ebury Press, London, 2016).

David Papineau, *Knowing the Score* (Constable, London, 2017).

David Peace, *The Damned United* (Faber & Faber, London, 2007).

David Peace, *Red or Dead* (Faber, London, 2013).

Thomas Nagel, 'What Is It Like to Be a Bat? *The Philosophical Review* 83 (4): pp. 435–50.

Pier Paolo Pasolini, *Les terrains: Écrits sur le sport* (Le temps des cerises, Paris, 2012).

Ted Richards (ed.), *Soccer and Philosophy* (Open Court, Chicago & La Salle, 2010).

Jean-Paul Sartre, *Critique of Dialectical Reason,* vol. 2 (Verso, London and New York, 1991).

Michel Serres, *The Parasite* (University of Minnesota Press, Minneapolis, 2007).

Paul Simpson and Uli Hesse, *Who Invented the Stepover?* (Profile Books, London, 2013).

Rob Steen, Jed Novick and Huw Richards, *The Cambridge Companion to Football* (Cambridge University Press, Cambridge, 2013).

David Stubbs, *Send Them Victorious: England's Path to Glory 2006-10* (Zero Books, Winchester, 2010).

Jean-Philippe Toussaint, *Football* (Fitzcarraldo, London, 2016).

Jonathan Wilson, *Inverting the Pyramid: The History of Football Tactics* (Orion, London, 2008).

Photo credits

Front endpaper: A boy heads a ball in front of a Messi mural in Kolkata, India, 2014. *DibyangshuSarkar/AFP/Getty Images*

p. v: World Cup Final, 1966. Jack Charlton falls to his knees in relief as Geoff Hurst (10) walks away with Martin Peters after completing his hat trick in the dying seconds. *Popperfoto*

p. vi: Marcel Desailly of Chelsea against Manchester United, March 1999. The game ended goalless. *Ben Radford/Allsport*

p. x: AC Milan's Ronaldinho attends a training session in Dubai, 2009. *Karim Sahib/AFP*

p. 3: Bill Shankly, practising his Wembley walk, 1973. *Evening Standard/Getty Images*

p. 8: Paul Breitner, who scored in the 1974 World Cup Final, when West Germany beat Holland 2-1, at the post-match banquet. *Rolls Press/Popperfoto/Getty Images*

p. 11: FIFA President Sepp Blatter names Qatar as the winning hosts of 2022 at the Messe Conference Centre in Zurich, 2010. *Laurence Griffiths/Getty Images*

p. 14: Diego Maradona of Argentina is confronted by a posse of Belgian defenders in the 1982 World Cup. Belgium marked Maradona zonally and won the game 1-0 *Steve Powell /Allsport*

p. 18: A Liverpool streaker on the pitch during the FA Cup match against Brighton & Hove Albion at Anfield, February 2012. *Paul Ellis/AFP/Getty Images*

p. 24: Roberto Firmino celebrates scoring Liverpool's second goal in a Premier League win at Stoke City, April 2017. The Greek script of his tattoo reads 'God is Faithful'. *Chris Brunskill Ltd/Getty Images*

p. 29: Thomas Mueller – Germany's space investigator. *Contrast/Ralf Pollack/ullstein bild via Getty Images*

p. 32: Laurent Blanc plants a kiss on the pate of French colleague Fabien Barthez before the Euro 2000 semi-final match against Portugal, June 2000. *Olivier Morin/AFP/Getty Images*

p. 40: Uruguay's Luis Suarez handballs in the last minute of extra time in the 2010 World Cup quarter-final against Ghana, July 2010, in Soweto, South Africa. Asamoah Gyan missed the penalty awarded and Uruguay went on to win the match on penalties. *Roberto Schmidt/AFP/Getty Images*

p. 46: Manchester City's German goalkeeper Bert Trautman keeping the balls in the air in training, 1951. Trautman was a former German POW who famously completed the 1956 FA Cup final for City with a broken neck; he helped City hang on to their 3-1 lead against Birmingham. *Popperfoto/Getty Images*

p. 50: Fireworks thrown onto the pitch by Galatasaray fans during a Champions League match against Borussia Dortmund, November 2014. *Martin Rose/Bongarts/Getty Images*

p. 57 Portuguese forward Eusebio celebrates after scoring a goal during a World Cup game against Bulgaria, 1966; Portugal won 3-0. *AFP/Getty Images*

p. 58: George Best celebrates after scoring Manchester United's second goal against Benfica in the 1968 European Cup Final; they won 4-1. *Popperfoto/Getty Images*

p. 64: Serbia & Montenegro fans raise the flag during the World Cup 2006 match against Argentina; their team, playing for the last time, lost 6-0. *Vladimir Rys/Bongarts/Getty Images*

p. 68: Barcelona's Cameroon forward Samuel Eto'o celebrates after winning the 2009 Spanish Cup final against Athletic Bilbao; Barcelona won 4-1. *Lluis Gene/AFP/Getty Images*

p. 72: Cristiano Ronaldo is injured during the 2016 European Championship Final between Portugal and France at the Stade de France. *Dave Winter/Icon Sport via Getty Images*

p. 78: Liverpool fans protest against the rise in ticket prices during a Premier League match against Sunderland at Anfield, February 2016. *Lindsey Parnaby/AFP/Getty Images*

p.83: Andrea Pirlo and Edinson Cavani exchange shirts during the 2014 World Cup Brazil Group D match between Italy and Uruguay in Natal, Brazil. *Julian Finney/Getty Images*

p. 86: Brian Clough managing Brighton, 1973. *Frank Tewkesbury/Evening Standard/Hulton Archive/Getty Images*

p. 94: Liverpool's John Barnes talks to manager Kenny Dalglish before a match against his old club, Watford, 1987; Liverpool won 4-0. *Bob Thomas/Getty Images*

p. 99: League One play-off semi final between Millwall and Scunthorpe Utd at The Den, 2017. *Mike Hewitt/Getty Images*

p. 102: A Swansea City supporter looks into the stadium before the Premier League match against AFC Bournemouth, December 2016. *Jordan Mansfield/Getty Images*

p. 108: Real's David Beckham consoles Zidane after he was sent off during a La Liga match against Villarreal at the Bernabeu, April 2005. Real won 2-1. *Denis Doyle/Getty Images*

p. 115: Zidane as Real Madrid manager at a La Liga match against Valencia, April 2017. *fotopress/Getty Images*

p. 120: Liverpool player Kenny Dalglish shares a talk with his manager Bob Paisley, March 1979. *Bob Thomas/Getty Images*

p. 127: After the Fall. Steven Gerrard contemplates the enormity of Chelsea scoring – and ending Liverpool's hopes of the Premier League at Anfield, 27 April 2014. *Clive Brunskill/Getty Images*

p. 134: Dortmund's coach Jürgen Klopp watches Bavarian musicians before a German Cup game with TSV 1860 Munich, September 2013. Christof *Stache/AFP/Getty Images*

p. 140: Arsenal's Clock End at Highbury, December 1951. *George Douglas/Picture Post/Getty Images*

p. 144: FA Cup Final, May 1972: Leeds United 1 v Arsenal 0. Norman Hunter leaps into the air to celebrate as Allan Clarke scores the winning goal. *Bob Thomas/Getty Images*

p. 152: Liverpool players and fans mob Dejan Lovren after he scores their fourth goal to seal their comeback against Borussia Dortmund in the UEFA Europa League quarter-final, April 2016. *Clive Brunskill/Getty Images*

p. 158: Russian President Vladimir Putin speaks as oligarch Chelsea owner Roman Abramovich looks on during a meeting with businessmen in Sochi, Russia, 2016. Putin said the latest report on doping among Russian athletes lacked substance. *Mikhail Svetlov/Getty Images*

p. 168: Ivorians celebrate as President Alassane Ouattara and Ivory Coast's midfielder Yaya Toure hold the 2015 African Cup of Nations trophy during a welcoming parade in Abidjan, February 2015. Ivory Coast had won the final against Ghana 9-8 on penalties. *Sia Kambou/AFP/Getty Images*

End endpaper: Johan Cruyff in a 1974 World Cup game for Holland against Uruguay; the Dutch won 2-0. *Bob Thomas/Getty Images*

Thanks

16 JANUARY 1998. Colchester, Essex, the old Layer Road ground. An exceptionally frigid evening. I took my son to see his first live football game. He was five years old. Colchester United versus Torquay United. Attendance 2776, which was not bad by Layer Road standards. 1-0 to Colchester. Tony Lock scored the winner. It was a terrible game. We had awful seats. But the importance of shit football should never be underestimated, of bad games between mediocre teams. Here you can see football culture at its purest: Colchester season ticket holders studying the programme intensely before the game, covered in scarves, hats, badges all over their jackets, greeting fellow fans, awaiting the game patiently and watching intently, but for the most part quietly, until one of their players makes a predictable error.

Back in the Vauxhall Corsa after the game, my son and I warmed up in the car park, listening to the radio. I asked him if he'd enjoyed the game. 'Yeah, I liked it.' I said, 'You wanna go again?' And we did, eventually graduating from Colchester United to Ipswich Town, who became our second team. Liverpool FC would always be first. I'd like to dedicate this book to my son, Edward, my constant companion in all matters related to football, and to the memory of my father, Bill, who died too young for my son to get to know him, but who taught me to play and with whom I learnt to think about football.

This book wouldn't have seen the light of day without Mark Ellingham, who – despite being a Manchester United supporter – is a very nice man. Mark's editing on this book has been remarkably helpful and I would also like to thank him for finding the images which accompany my text. Because of Mark, I was very fortunate to get feedback from David Goldblatt and Paul Simpson and their incisive comments on an earlier version of this book proved invaluable, as did some crucial remarks by Natania Jansz. Miles Ellingham did some really great work on image research and found many fascinating photos. I'd also like to thank the following for their help with this project: Ridvan Askin, Lucas Ballestin, Philip Schauss, David Buckley, Hugh Eakin, Colin Robinson, Nemonie Craven, Rosie Welsh, Jacques Testard, Hal Foster, Sandy Tait, Sina Najafi and Ida Lødemel Tvedt.

Index

Italic page references indicate illustrations; an 'n' refers to the numbered endnotes between pages 172 and 176.

Leeds United 85, 88, 97, 122, *144–5*, 170n22
Lefkowitz, Mary 95, 171n23
Leicester City 4, 71, 123
Liedholm, Niels 33
Liverpool Football Club
    2013-14 season 126
    2015-16 season 129
    author's family commitment
        to 19–20, 35
    historic achievements
        88–9, 126, 142
    Liverpool v Borussia
        Dortmund 139,
        149, *152–3*,
        172n28
    Liverpool v Chelsea 126,
        127
    Liverpool v Everton 36
    Liverpool v Watford *94*
    Manchester United taunts
        97, 100
    'Self-Righteous Liverpool
        Supporter' 128
    'the Shirt' 128, 130, 142
    see also Klopp; Shankly
Lovren, Dejan 150, *152–3*

M

magazines 23
magic and superstition 33–4
Mainz, FSV 125
Maldini, Paolo 13, 28
managers, depiction of 119, 162
Manchester City *46*, 126
Manchester United *vi*, 6, *58*,
    71, 97, 100, 103, 129
Mane, Sadio 155
Maradona, Diego *14*, 42

Marx, Karl, *Capital* 7, 170n3
Marxism 7, 12
Materazzi, Marco 117
mediated reality 48–9, 59, 92,
    107, 113, 166
Merleau-Ponty, Maurice 15,
    30, 38
    The Structure of Behaviour
        30, 171n12
Merseyside derbies 36
Messi, Lionel 6, 49, *end*
    endpaper
Middle Kingdom 47–8
Milan, A C *x*, 28, 33, 89, 123,
    151, *end endpaper*
Milan, Inter *182*
Millwall *98–9*
Milner, James 150
mimetic events 55, 59, 76
mind, disengagement 44
Modern Tragedy, by Raymond
    Williams 174n32
moments
    creation of 132, 138, 169
    history of 137, 138, 151
    moment of vision 132,
        136–7, 173–4n27
money
    and the form of football
        157, 167
    growing influence of 9–10,
        119
'moneyball' transfer policy 126
Montenegro 63, *64*, 65
moral function, alleged
    of argument between fans
        104
    of theatre and football
        80–1
More, Thomas, *Utopia* 88

Z